FRANK PARKER

HAVILAH PRESS • CHICAGO

CYNTHIA BEARDSLEY

FRANK PARKER

Champion
in the Golden Age
of Tennis

Frank Parker: Champion in the Golden Age of Tennis

© Copyright 2002 by Cynthia Beardsley

Havilah Press
858 W. Armitage, #242
Chicago, Illinois 60614
cbeardsley@iols.net

Designer: Diane Jaroch, Diane Jaroch Design, Rockford, IL
Editor: Mary Edsey, Tabagio Press, Chicago, IL

Printed in Singapore.
First printing 2002.

10 9 8 7 6 5 4 3 2 1

Publisher's Cataloging in Publication Data

Beardsley, Cynthia
Frank Parker – Champion in the Golden Age of Tennis
Includes 118 pages, index, appendix, and list of illustrations.
ISBN 0-9705449-7-9

1. Parker, Frank
2. Tennis players - United States
Biography

Library of Congress Control Number: 2001094522
796.342

In memory of Frank Parker—

my tennis coach, mentor, and friend.

Contents

Chapter One

BOY WONDER

Chapter Two

A GENTLEMAN'S
SPORT

Chapter Three

RISE TO
STARDOM

Though tennis great Frank Parker led a quiet, subdued, and dignified life, his tennis racket made noise throughout the world. He captivated not only tennis fans, who idolized his classic style and impeccable attire, but also women, who considered his legs the best looking on tour.

His was an era of wooden rackets, weary non-air travel, and meager expenses in which most players were true sportsmen. Frank never questioned a call or argued with an umpire, but opponents hated him on the court as he relentlessly and expressionlessly took them apart like a cool experienced knife fighter. Between matches, however, Frank's adversaries admired his quiet reserved manner and never questioned his authoritative tennis wisdom. He would show up for a match, clobber his opponent, sing in good voice as he showered, and return home with his wife, Audrey, to their patiently waiting cat. Frank had little outward demeanor, and few could figure him out.

Many contended his tennis game was vulnerable with a suspect hitch in his forehand. However, Frankie's forehand always seemed to hold up under attack, allowing his backhand to penetrate his opponent's court as if he were a shooter in a shooting gallery. Playing in today's tennis market Frank would surely be a major prizewinner.

Frank Parker's biography is the story of a man who had an unusual, exciting, and successful life of boyhood tennis, national championships, Davis Cup participation, and World War II adventure. He was Mr. Tennis—a legend in his own time.

Gardnar Mulloy

Gardnar Mulloy and Frank Parker served together as members of the U.S. Davis Cup team in 1946 and 1948. They were also major rivals in numerous singles and doubles matches throughout their tennis careers— Frank being the victor ninety-nine percent of the time. Mulloy was inducted into the International Tennis Hall of Fame in 1972. He now resides in Miami, Florida.

I met Frank Parker in 1990 when I began taking tennis lessons from him at the McClurg Court Sports Center in downtown Chicago. I particularly enjoyed Frank's great sense of humor during my lessons. He always made me laugh with witty expressions, such as "higher Meyer" when my serve didn't make it over the net. We became close friends and continued to play tennis together for the next seven years.

It was Frank's idea to write this book. I had just completed my masters degree in history in June of 1996, when Frank asked me if I would write his biography. I was honored and agreed to take on the task. A few days later Frank was at my door with bags of articles and photographs. I spent weeks sorting them chronologically. Over the next several months I met Frank every other week to discuss the book's progress.

In July of 1997 Frank became ill and died shortly thereafter. He never saw the completed manuscript. I continued the project after his death as a tribute to a man who had been not only my tennis instructor but a very dear friend.

I would like to thank my editor, Mary Edsey of Tabagio Press, for her time, effort, and hard work, and for guiding me through the self-publishing process and helping me get the book finished. Thank you to Diane Jaroch for her outstanding design work. Heartfelt thanks to Gardnar Mulloy for writing the introduction. Special thanks to Barbara Vuletic of Evergreen Racquet and Fitness Club for supplying several of the photos, and to Tulane archivist Robert Sherer for information regarding Frank's school years. Many thanks to Dorothy Ash for her interview and to the following tennis players for taking the time to be interviewed: Pancho Segura, Ted Schroeder, Tony Trabert, Gene Mako, Eddie Moylan, Cliff Sutter, and Bill Talbert.

Preface

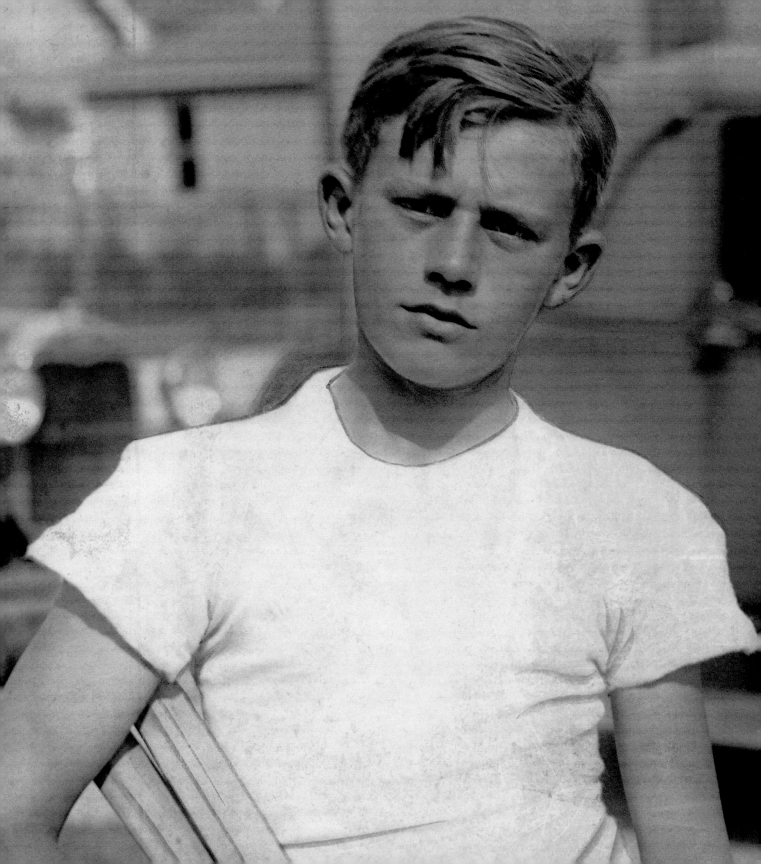

Chapter One

BOY

WONDER

"François, how good to see you this evening. Your table is waiting."

"The service is always so slow here," the smiling gentleman jokingly replied as the maitre d' waved him past a queue of patrons.

The man's alluring good looks, impeccable dress, and confident stride seemed to set the restaurant aglow with his charm. His well-tailored suit accented his trim physique. His pocket handkerchief matched not only his silk tie but his ice-blue eyes, which met the glance of many a woman as he waltzed to his corner booth.

"I'll bet your name is as beautiful as you are," he flirted to the cocktail waitress. While shaking the hands of admiring men, who stopped to acknowledge his achievements, he cheerfully replied, "A pleasure to meet you."

Though handsomely disguised, his eighty years and bygone fame were proudly revealed by his ever-present lapel pin—"Davis Cup, 1937," "Dinah Shore Tournament," and "Robert Kennedy Memorial Tournament" were but a few from his vast collection. He was Frank Parker, known to tennis fans of the 30s and 40s as the "Boy Wonder of Tennis"—winner of over 100 titles from his first amateur victory at a local Milwaukee tournament at the age of eleven to his last professional victory at the 1949 Pan-American Championships in Mexico at the age of thirty-three.

Franciszek Andrzej Paikowski, a.k.a. Frank A. Parker, was born in Milwaukee, Wisconsin, on January 31, 1916, the youngest of five children of Paul and Anna Dzemenske Paikowski. Paul, a hard-working employee of the Water Department of Milwaukee, was a devoted husband and loving father. He died when Frank was only two years old. Anna never remarried and bravely supported her large family and her mother on income she earned laundering clothes. A devoutly religious woman, Anna attended 6:00 AM Mass every morning with her children.

In contrast to their means, Frank and his siblings, John, Sylvester, Tony, and Genevieve, all managed to discover tennis at an exclusive local

The Paikowski children: *(clockwise from upper left)* Tony, John, Sylvester, Jean, and Francis.

country club called the Milwaukee Town Club. Built on the city's Gold Coast in 1903 at the corner of Farwell and Brady Street and frequent host of the Wisconsin Open, the private club attracted a wealthy clientele and offered the Parker children an opportunity to earn some money.

John Parker, Frank's oldest brother, worked as the country club manager. Though the position gave him the opportunity to excel on the squash courts, it also gave his little brother Frank his first exposure to tennis at the age of eight. Along with two of his brothers, who also strung rackets at home for club members, Frank got his first job at the club "shagging" wild tennis balls on the courts for two dollars a week.

Frank instantly fell in love with the game. He would sneak onto the tennis courts every chance he had. There were no indoor tennis courts at the time, so in the winter when the courts were iced-over for skating, Frank would practice tennis on the indoor squash courts and ice skate on the tennis courts just to stay flexible. By the age of ten his unyielding passion for the sport had already nurtured his unmistakable talent—a talent that would not go unnoticed.

Milwaukeean E. A. "Ted" Bacon, a recreational tennis player and wealthy executive of the Cutler Hammer Foundation, had a profound love for the game of tennis. He also understood that competitive tennis was a rich man's game, which left many talented players out of the competition. Bacon noticed Frank playing at the club and became extremely interested in helping him succeed.

In the summer of 1926 Ted Bacon requested that Mercer Beasley, a tennis coach from Pasadena, California, with an international reputation, be hired as tennis pro at the Town Club in hopes that he could train young Frank. Beasley coached many well-known players, who would go on to greater fame, including Ellsworth Vines (U.S. Nationals champion–1931, 1932; Wimbledon champion–1932), Cliff Sutter (national intercollegiate champion from Tulane University–1930, 1932), Wilmer Allison (U.S. Nationals doubles

Young Frank Parker practicing his backhand.

champion with Johnny Van Ryn–1931, 1935; Wimbledon champion–1929, 1930), Bitsy Grant (Davis Cup team member–1935, 1936, 1937), and Doris Hart (winner of all twelve major titles—a record only she and Margaret Court held among male and female players). In all, Mercer Beasley's trainees would win over eighty-four national titles.

Beasley's philosophy was that "tennis players were bred, not born, to greatness." In his new position at the club he was anxious to experiment with this theory by training a young protégé who had no prior lessons or bad habits. Beasley had a vision of molding a tennis player to win through strategy rather than hard-hitting, as Bill Tilden was then doing. He believed that Frank not only fit the category but had the ambition and desire to excel.

Over the next several months Mercer Beasley worked diligently with Frank. His instructional method seemed to suit Frank's style, as the young boy began to perfect his game. Beasley's conservative coaching applied strict guidelines he would later include in his 1933 book *How to Play Tennis: The Beasley System*. He instructed Frank to keep his eye on the ball and anticipate its direction. He insisted that the racket be held with one hand, never two, and rested on the shoulder before backhand and forehand shots. Frank was also taught not to talk or show emotion on the court, as Beasley's book reads, "Avoid making any gestures or audible sounds that might cause comment."[1] He was put on a strict nutritional diet, a tight sleeping schedule, and a rigorous practice regimen, leaving him no time to socialize with friends.

In July of 1927, just months after Beasley shaped Frank's game, the eleven-year-old earned his first victory in the Wisconsin Open Championships at the Milwaukee Town Club. Frank had entered the tournament two years earlier on his own and made it to the quarterfinals, despite being the youngest entrant.

Frank attended Saint Hedwig's Catholic School from kindergarten through sixth grade. In 1928 Ted Bacon came through again for Frank by offering to underwrite the boy's enrollment and tennis expenses at the Mil-

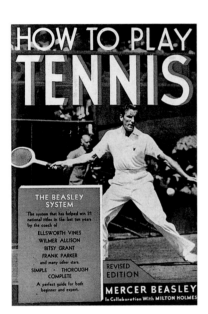

Mercer Beasley's
1933 instruction book,
*How to Play Tennis:
The Beasley System,*
relays the conservative
coaching style he
applied to Frank.

While under the
tutelage of acclaimed
coach Mercer Beasley,
Frank began his
early exposure to the
rich and famous.

Above: Frank with
Coach Beasley, and
actor Frederic March.

Right: Frank and tennis
champion Bill Tilden.

waukee Country Day School, known for its tennis squad. Frank attended the school with Bacon's funding until 1930. However, he was not allowed to play on the school's Country Day Tennis Squad. The school had quickly realized that Frank's game was in a league of its own and felt that including him would be harmful to the competitive spirit of the interschool games.

This did not discourage Frank. For three hours every day after school, he worked on his game, tuning a backhand that eventually would become one of the finest in tennis.

It was Frank's forehand that would see numerous changes over the years as Beasley tried to perfect the stroke. In a 1972 tennis anthology, sports writer George McGann would remark, "Each spring, as the buds blossomed and the birds flew north, sports writers all over the country would speculate on the new Forehand Model. There was always a hitch in the wind-up, and nothing that Beas or Parker ever tried would eliminate it. One year, the New Model, had absolutely no wind-up; another year the forehand resembled a side-arm delivery in baseball…"[2]

The accuracy, timing, and speed of Frank's shots enabled him to practice with top members of the Milwaukee Town Club. In the winter of 1928 Frank was in southern California practicing for upcoming matches when 23-year-old Helen Wills (Moody), seven-time Wimbledon champion, was playing at the same club. Beasley wanted Frank to play a set with her, but Helen Wills was not interested in being challenged by a twelve-year-old. However, after seeing Frank perform in a game of doubles, she consented. Frank beat Wills in the first three sets. They tied 7-all in the fourth, and Wills finally pulled ahead 9-7. She was so impressed by Frank's accuracy and quickness that she offered to play him again any time.[3]

Frank spent his first year of high school at the Black Fox Military Academy in Los Angeles, but transferred his second year to Fourtier High School in New Orleans. Mercer Beasley was the pro at nearby Tulane University and wanted to continue coaching this promising young player.

Anna Paikowski wishes well to her young athletic son.

Beasley's coaching style is described in the school's 1934 yearbook: "A large part of the Wave's success on the courts in 1933 can be attributed to the new kind of tennis practice (begun by Beasley). Believing that to be a tennis player of any repute one had to be an all-around athlete and have a physique strong enough to give him the maximum efficiency in every stroke, Beasley had Tulane's tennis aspirants exercising every afternoon in regular gymnasium classes… including running, jumping, practicing strats on the cinder path, winding up their work with several laps around the track."[4]

The coach expected this same strict routine of his young protégé and had his wife, Audrey, watch over Frank to ensure it. Tulane tennis star Cliff Sutter recalled Frank's years under Beasley's tutelage, "Frank was a very attractive person. While practicing at Tulane, all of the wealthy families of New Orleans wanted to invite Frank over for dinner to meet their daughters. However, Mrs. Beasley forbade it. Locals often asked me what was going on with him. Audrey traveled with Frank and held on to him. She had a strict schedule for Frank, and she had her eyes on him. Frank could have married into major money in New Orleans but never had the chance." Some years later the *Milwaukee Journal* reported, "She [Audrey] generally travels with Frankie and supervises his diet during tournaments."[5]

In 1933 when Beasley took a job at his alma mater, Lawrenceville School in New Jersey, Frank transferred to the large prestigious prep school, and Beasley financed his education. As star of the Lawrenceville tennis team, Frank competed against high school teams such as Hill, Choate, and Andover, and college players at Yale and Princeton. He also participated in the Princeton Interscholastic (champion–1934, 1935) and Bermuda Interscholastic (champion–1937) school tournaments. Frank never lost a match in school tennis. From 1934 to 1936 he was elected captain of the tennis squad and held a record for the most matches won.[6]

Frank transferred to Fourtier High School in New Orleans his second year so he could continue his training with Beasley, who was coaching at nearby Tulane University.

Right: Frank never lost a tennis match while attending Lawrenceville School in New Jersey.

Far right: Frank, Coach Beasley, and teammate Winship Nunnally.

Photos: Lawrenceville School yearbook

YEAR	MATCHES PLAYED	GAMES WON	GAMES LOST	PERCENTAGE
1934	9	108	14	.885
1935	8	96	11	.897
1936	18	108	13	.893

While attending Lawrenceville, Frank did not confine his activities to tennis. He was an all-around athlete who golfed, jogged, and played baseball in the summer and boxed, ran track, and played basketball (for which he received a varsity letter) in the winter. He also wrote poetry and sketched. Yet Frank was lonely and missed his family, so he also kept himself occupied on various Lawrenceville committees: the Class Day Committee, Student Council, and Glee Club. He was also co-president of the Cleve House, one of the famous Lawrenceville "circle" dormitories.

If Frank had not moved away to fulfill his tennis career, he would have taken a blue collar job in Milwaukee to help contribute to his family's financial needs. Frank's siblings all worked and helped out, but because this was the amateur pre-open era, Frank did not make any money and could not contribute to the family's finances.

His financial situation was similar to that of many amateur tennis players of his era—the depression and wartime forties. Those who were not wealthy were supported by wealthy tennis buffs. They learned on public courts but were invited to play at private clubs and participate in exclusive tournaments. They couldn't afford to stay at hotels but were often asked to stay in the homes of hosting families.

Although disappointed to see her young son leave home, Anna was delighted that he had such a rare opportunity. She was, however, deeply hurt by an erroneous newspaper story suggesting that Frank had been legally adopted by Mercer Beasley. "The Beasleys made no secret of the fact that they regarded Frank as their own son. Their attempt to adopt him was dropped when Mrs. Paikowski objected. She said she couldn't give up her boy," the *Milwau-*

III.

Well, here is the poem I promised. It took me all week. It may interest you
to know that we are studying poetry and one day this week the urge hit me to
write a poem. So here you have I. Take it for what it is worth.

The sea separates us,

But I can tell-as I lay my head on the pillow,

That all is well.

Remember the parting day on the dock?

As we cried and the boat rocked.

My heart fell for you that cold day- I confess.

What a shame we can't continue-our happiness.

Oh, my heart pines for you this day,

Poor me, and you so far away.

Your letters cross the great sea,

They bring me much news from thee.

I dream on your letters every night,

They are such a comfort to me-allright.

As the bell rings to go to bed-I simply lay awake and dream of

the past summer's delight.

Don't fret when things look bad,

You may not believe me, but it makes me sad.

I wish I were there to take you in my arms,

And hold you, until you whispered "Be calm".

With love and kisses,

Andzej

kee Journal stated.[7] "Frankie is still my son, and Mr. Beasley has never been more than his coach and manager," Anna retorted.[8]

Anna was very proud of Frank. She kept scrapbooks of his newspaper articles and displayed his trophies and photographs prominently in their Milwaukee home at 1314 E. Hamilton Avenue. Money was tight, but Frank's family attended his matches in Milwaukee and Chicago.

Frank was only fourteen when he won his first national title at the 1930 U.S. Boys' Championships doubles tournament with George Boynton. The following year Frank took the title at the U.S. Boys' Championships singles tournament, defeating Gene Mako (7-5, 8-6).

In 1932 he again defeated Mako in the U.S. Junior Championships singles tournament (6-8, 3-6, 6-1, 9-7, 6-2) and became the number one junior player. "Parker was seeded at the top of the draw and was the heavy favorite. The choice was not wrong, for Mercer Beasley's young protégé displayed remarkable tournament strength, poise that would have done credit to a player twice his age, and consummate skill in all departments of the game," reported *American Lawn Tennis* magazine. "Frank elected to play from the baseline, sweeping the corners and using a steady change of pace."[9] Mako still recalls, "Frank's best weapon was his consistency."

Frank eventually became one of only two men (the other being Joe Hunt) to have won the U.S. Boys' Championships title (1931), the U.S. Junior Championships title (1932), and the U.S. Nationals title (1944, 1945).

In 1932 Frank made his first of nineteen appearances at the U.S. Nationals (currently the U. S. Open) at Forest Hills, New York. He excelled in the first and second round, but lost to George Lott in the third round (6-4, 6-1, 4-6, 6-2). In the same year he defeated Lott in the Canadian Championships men's singles, a title won by few Americans, and claimed his first senior title. Lott wrote, "The early rounds of the singles went off without any upsets, the feature being the champion-to-be's machine-like play. He went through his matches losing very few games and making very few errors. It was

A FAMILY GROUP AT SOUTHAMPTON
Mr and Mrs Mercer Beasley and "Frankie" Parker, snapped when the finals at the Meadow Club were over

Audrey and Mercer Beasley took such a liking to young Frank that a photo caption appearing in American Lawn tennis on August 20, 1935, referred to them as "a family."

Frank's mom proudly displayed his trophies in their Milwaukee home.

Photo: The Milwaukee Journal

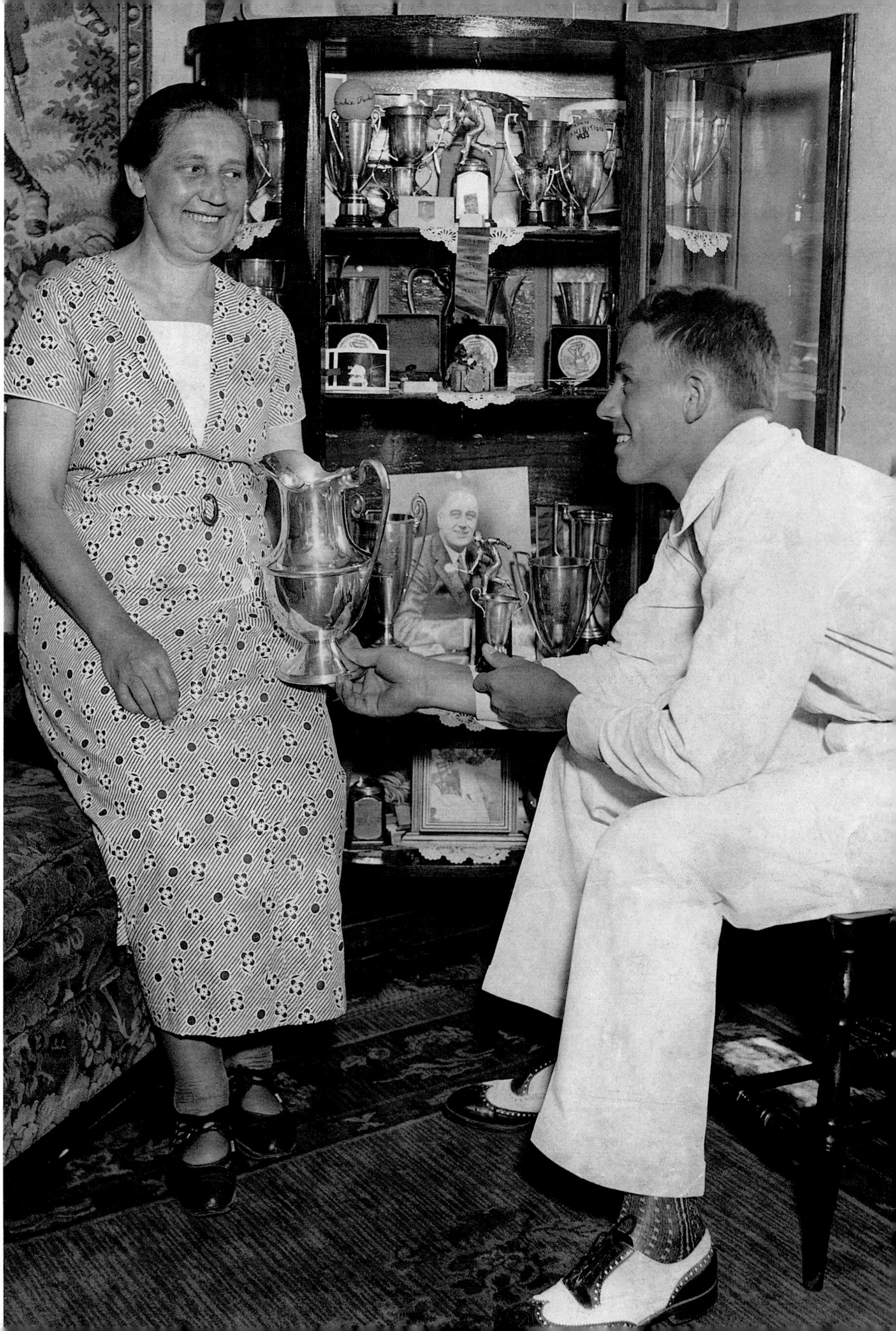

Frank made his first
of nineteen appearances
at the U.S. Nationals
in Forest Hills, New York,
in 1932.

Photo: Associated Press

Photo: Geoffrey Landesman

slightly reminiscent of the way Tilden used to wade through his first round matches."[10]

By the following year Frank had grown two inches and gained ten pounds. "…he is hitting much harder and seems to have lost none of his uncanny ability to find the openings in his opponent's court. Both ground strokes and volleys are hit with a crispness and certainty that gives his opponent no time to get set for shots. His serve is also greatly improved. While he usually plays practically on the base line he sometimes takes a deep shot by advancing toward the net and volleying with great speed from behind the service line and quite close to the ground, still getting very effective angles," *American Lawn Tennis* reported of his win at the Kentucky State Championships in June.[11]

During that year Frank was ranked for the first time in the USLTA's top ten, and continued to be ranked there for the next seventeen consecutive years—a record only beaten by Jimmy Connors' eighteenth and nineteenth consecutive wins in 1988 and 1989. (Bill Larned was ranked in the top ten for nineteen years between 1892 and 1911, but not consecutively.)

Frank's speed, agility, quick hands at the net, and ability to cover the court in three strides soon earned him the nickname "Boy Wonder of Tennis." He won every tournament with finesse, accuracy, perfect timing, and sound footwork. "Cool, though far from indifferent to the play, he is hard to rattle. There is seldom a frown on his forehead, and his gray eyes see no farther than the white stripes that bound his place de combat," commented *Milwaukee Journal* reporter Edward Hart. "And that 'poker face' has helped to wear down more than one of Frank's opponents, particularly those who are inclined to be temperamental. In all the times I have seen him play he has never uttered more than a faint squeal, and had I not been watching every move, I should not have known whether he was pleased or piqued."[12]

Frank described his own game in a 1935 biographical sketch form sent to *American Lawn Tennis* magazine, "Use three grips on forehand—Eastern, Western and Continental; two on backhand. All-court game, prefer my opponent to take the net. Rather play base line game and hold to the basic principle as taught to me by Mercer Beasley that accuracy is far more important than speed. Practice accurate play, always having an exact place for the ball to go. Service best on second ball, and I win more points on the second ball than on the first. I make no change of speed."[13]

In 1936 Frank graduated from Lawrenceville School. He had the opportunity to attend Princeton but decided to forego college and devote his time to tennis. Frank received his real education by traveling around the world on the tennis circuit. His lifestyle changed dramatically from living in the poor Polish district on the northeast side of Milwaukee. He traveled to far away places and across the class lines of society. Yet he did not let his new lifestyle and success go to his head but remained modest and unassuming.

When Mercer Beasley was too busy coaching other players, his wife, Audrey, would often accompany Frank to tournaments. Tennis player Pancho Segura recalls, "Frank was a favorite with the ladies. Beasley sent his wife, Audrey, with Frank to look after him and to keep the women away from Frank when he was traveling to tournaments. Frank was so attractive that Beasley did not want Frank to leave with a gal. Beasley was afraid that Frank would lose his main focus on tennis. The girls would jump at Frank any time they got the chance."

In 1936 the United States Government chose Frank Parker, then twenty years of age, to be a goodwill ambassador to Europe for three months. Audrey Beasley accompanied Frank on the trip.

A

GENTLEMAN'S

SPORT

In Frank's heyday of the 1930s and 40s, competitive tennis was a far different sport than it is today. Players were less compensated, audiences more sophisticated, travel less accommodating, and attire more conservative.

Players wore white shoes, white socks, long white pants or skirts, and white shirts or blouses without labels or logos. A sports jacket with a handkerchief in the pocket became Frank Parker's trademark wardrobe after every tournament. His attire on the court was initially long white pants or knickers, "knickerbockers," tied just below the knee, but Frank soon decided the pants were uncomfortable and began wearing his track running shorts instead. Though the English amateur Bunny Austin was the first player to wear shorts in a tournament, Frank Parker was the first American amateur to do so. He debuted the outfit in 1937 during the Davis Cup at Wimbledon. Authorities attempted to ban him from the competition unless he changed into appropriate clothing, but Frank called their bluff and was eventually allowed to play.

American Lawn Tennis reported, "The very abbreviated American shorts worn by Parker and Grant caused comment in the English press, and some amusement amongst the spectators. Of course, it never occurred to them that the long dignified and carefully pleated English type shorts (as worn by Bunny Austin) seem quite as odd to American galleries. Frank Parker, wearing these short shorts and pouring ice water down his neck during his match with Bunny Austin on a day that was far from warm, made many a spectator shiver."[14]

Frank's youth and great legs warded off complaints from fans. However, when older players later began to follow suit, tennis clubs received numerous phone calls of disgust.

At $7 a pair, tennis shoes of the day did not provide the same comfort as today's heavily-cushioned $75 variety. As a result most players, including Frank, fought bad blisters on the tennis court through much of their careers. At the Pacific Southwest Championships in 1948, Frank defaulted a match due to blisters, even though he was leading Ted Schroeder (6-4, 9-7, 5-7). In his later years Frank relished the luxury of comfortable tennis shoes.

Rackets of the era were wooden and cost about twenty-five dollars. Not surprisingly, Frank chose Spalding's "Mercer Beasley" model. Until Wilson's "Jack Kramer" racket came on the market in 1947, "Mercer Beasley" was the best-selling racket of the 1930s and 40s.

Almost every tournament in the era was played on grass or clay courts. Frank recalled that although players enjoyed the improved serves and volleys of grass courts, most preferred clay courts because of the unpredictable ball bounces on grass.

Tennis audiences were also different. People who attended the matches were high society, sophisticated, well-mannered, and conservatively dressed. The United States Lawn Tennis Association (USLTA, currently the USTA), the governing organization of U.S. amateur tennis, seemed to have its own reputation for bias along economic and class lines. Tennis champion Alice Marble wrote in 1947, "On the whole I believe the USLTA to be a fair-minded, constructive organization… There is an element however which does not belong in this fine game of ours—one of snobbery which one senses but cannot pin down to actual facts. Some of the officials expect the players to cater in order to be invited into the closely-knit clique of the USLTA."[15]

Tennis itself was more of a gentleman's game. Players never cussed or threw their rackets. The relationship between players was friendlier. There were no antics—the game was strictly tennis. Frank said that not trying was the worst thing a player would do then. If a performance was not strong, fans would say the player "tanked it."

Though professional tennis attire has remained conservative, it has become much more comfortable for players since Frank's day. (American Lawn Tennis, May 1949, 43 and June 1949, 26.)

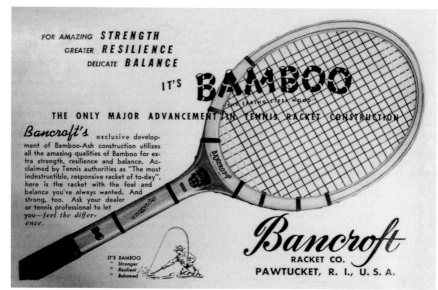

Frank used to watch his opponents during matches to study their games, unlike today's players who can study themselves and other players on videotape. Frank and his opponents were amateurs. Some players did not have coaches—much less agents or secretaries like the professionals do today. They played because they loved tennis, winning tournaments, and receiving trophies. If a player did not earn a high ranking, he would probably not be invited to the next tournament.

No money was awarded. None of the players had commercial sponsors—they were not allowed. The USLTA did, however, allow players to accept a maximum of $10 per day for expenses incurred in seventeen tournaments—four national championships, five sectional championships, and eight other tournaments. The organization often turned a blind eye to reporting illegitimate expenses, "chiseling," for such things as the hotel expenses of players who had been guests in private homes. Sports editor R. G. Lynch wrote, "To have much chance in top-notch competition, a tennis player must put in a lot of tournament play. This is no problem if the player has well fixed parents or

an 'angel.'... Of course, a man must live between tournaments, so the amateur code of tennis, despite USLTA's policy, would make it pretty much a rich man's sport were it not for the hypocritical attitude which has existed toward chiseling."[16]

Many amateur players also received money "under the table" to persuade them to participate in one tournament over another. It was not until years later that television and advertising turned tennis into a lucrative sport.

Today players travel thousands of miles a year by plane to compete in various tournaments around the world. In Frank's day less refined modes of transportation made competitive tennis much more difficult. Players traveled to tournaments by car, boat, or propeller plane. Traveling to England for one tournament meant a four-day trip on the Queen Mary cruise ship from New York and a four-day return trip on the Queen Elizabeth. Players would make good use of the time and stay in shape by playing ping-pong, running on the decks, or swimming. Cliff Sutter recalled, "Most players never traveled to Australia via the steamer, and very few ventured to Europe. The travel would take several days, and you would have 'sea legs' for at least a week after the trip. It would take up the whole summer, and the most important U.S. tournaments were held then."

Most major tennis events were held during only five months of the year so players would not get burned out from the exhausting travel. This allowed them to hold odd jobs in the off-season. Frank worked at the Santa Anna racetrack counting tickets, and at a Los Angeles department store, Broadway, as a salesperson.

Coaching in the 1930s was also quite conservative. Mercer Beasley's popular instruction book for beginners gave advice most players would find laughable today: "Not an action of yours should show elation or dejection. Nothing he does, whether it be to score an ace or to make an error, should change your expression." "Go to bed by 10 o'clock, ten hours of sleep will do you no harm." "If you must smoke, smoke as little as possible. Make it a definite rule never to smoke in your tennis clothing." "Once out on the court, there must be no fussing or adjusting of straps, belts, or anything else. White is generally worn. Indeed, the wearing of white is considered only courteous, in that color of any kind distracts the eye. Wear flat-soled rubber sneakers… Heels, no matter how low, cause twisted and sprained ankles."[17]

Beasley's advice was well heeded by Frank. On the September 8, 1942 "Bill Stern's Sport Show," the newscaster commented, "At first Frank Parker was laughed at because he was probably the most colorless tennis player who ever walked on a tennis court. He was a skinny chap with a serious face who never smiled, and who only came on a tennis court to play tennis. He never clowned, never acted up for the gallery. He never made himself a colorful attraction."

But Beasley's strict training put Frank Parker on a path toward championship. George McGann writes in *The Fireside Book of Tennis,* "The most important traits instilled into Parker by his mentor were the ability to devote himself completely to tennis, to play the game without ever being disturbed by outside factors, and the wonderful quality of perfect sportsmanship. Parker was the ideal opponent. There was never any 'incident' in a match in which he played. He just went about the business of winning. Frank's serious attitude was in part the result of Beas' insistence that nothing should interfere with a businesslike attention to the game."[18]

And in *Tennis: It's History, People and Events,* author Will Grimsley writes, "… Parker achieved fame through hard work and dedication. Under Beasley's watchful eye, Parker drilled himself hours at a time until he was able to hit a serve on a dime and knock a forehand drive through a twelve-inch hole. He lacked the big guns of his opponents but usually leveled them with rapid rifle fire."[19]

TO

RISE

Once Frank began competing on the tennis circuit, it took little time for him to become a national champion. His rising success was exemplified by his total domination of the Spring Lake tournament in New Jersey, where he was called "the sun-bronzed lad from out of the West."[20] The tournament was a high society event held at the Spring Lake Bathing and Tennis Club (now known as the Spring Lake Bath and Tennis Club) in its heyday as a fashionable summer resort from the 1920s through the 40s.

"Located 60 miles from New York, Spring Lake has been made famous through the years by the generous hospitality of Clifford Hemphill, president of the Bathing and Lawn Tennis Club," *American Lawn Tennis* reported. "The main 'grass' activity, as always, is the wide lawn of the Hemphill estate, where popular host, Clifford Hemphill and his family, hold their annual cocktail party at the conclusion of the meet. And where, as always, the two Hemphill grandsons stole the show from the mighty athletes by taking the baton from the orchestra leader and conducting the music."[21]

The ocean setting made this Frank's favorite tournament. He succeeded like no one else at Spring Lake, winning the event ten of the thirteen years that it was held from 1933 to 1949. (The tournament was canceled from 1942 to 1945.) In the club's 100th anniversary booklet writer Kevin Coyle recalls Frank's skill at the event, "His cross-court backhand drives rocketed diagonally from baseline to baseline, and kept his opponents skidding helplessly in pursuit."[22]

In 1933 Frank defeated Frank Shields (6-4, 6-4, 6-2); in 1934 Cliff Sutter (11-9, 6-1, 2-6, 6-2); in 1935 Charles Harris (8-6, 6-4, 6-0); in 1936 Bobby Riggs (6-2, 6-4, 7-5); in 1938 Archie Henderson (6-3, 6-3, 6-3); in 1939 Gardnar Mulloy (6-0, 6-4, 6-2); in 1940 Gardnar Mulloy (6-1, 6-3, 6-4); in 1941 Wayne Sabin (2-6, 0-6, 6-1, 6-3, 6-3); in 1946 Gardnar Mulloy (6-2, 6-3, 6-2); and in 1949 Bill Talbert (3-6, 7-5, 6-4, 6-0). Frank did not play in 1937 or 1948 because he was competing in European tournaments.

The first player to win the tournament three times was awarded the Hemphill Bowl, a Tiffany sterling trophy then valued at $5,000 and donated by the club's president Clifford Hemphill. Frank was awarded the bowl in 1935, 1939, and 1946.

Gardnar Mulloy confessed, "Few people remember Frank Parker's incredible string of wins at Spring Lake, New Jersey. I do, because I was his victim in several finals. It is said Frank never lost a set there, as his coach Mercer Beasley, the resident pro, forbid it.

It's a sore spot to discuss Frank's scores against me, as it's too embarrassing. I prefer to talk about my only win over him accomplished at the fabulous River Oaks Championships in Houston. As great a player as Frankie was, he did, like all champions, lose on rare occasions proving he was human."

Frank's only defeat at Spring Lake was to Eddie Moylan in the semifinals in 1947. Moylan recalled, "Frank Parker was one of the great, great players I have played and one of the finest gentlemen ever. He reminded me of royalty when he stepped on the court. When you won a point from Frank, you deserved it. There were no easy points with him."

The Spring Lake doubles matches also awarded a sterling trophy, donated by Frederic L. Duggan, secretary of the Spring Lake Bathing and Tennis Club. Frank won the men's doubles tournament six times: in 1934 with Johnny Van Ryn defeating Greg Mangin and Berkeley Bell (7-5, 5-7, 6-4, 6-2); in 1935 with Gil Hall defeating Wilbur Hess and Hal Surface (6-3, 3-6, 6-2, 6-4); in 1938 with Wilmer Allison defeating Charles Hare and Eugene McCauliff (6-0, 6-1); in 1939 with Gene Mako defeating Frank Shields and John Doeg (6-0, 6-4, 6-3); in 1946 with Gardnar Mulloy defeating Don McNeill and Frank Guernsey (4-6, 6-4, 5-7, 6-4, 6-3); and in 1947 with Gardnar Mulloy defeating Bill Talbert and Frank Guernsey (6-3, 6-4, 6-4).

Another tour that Frank dominated was the men's national singles title in the U.S. Clay Court Championships, which he won in Illinois in 1933, 1939, 1941, 1946, and 1947. In 1939 Frank also won the championships' men's doubles title with Gene Mako. Frank conquered the Eastern Clay Court Championships as well, winning in 1940, 1941, 1946, 1947, and 1948.

Clifford Hemphill presents Frank with his first Hemphill Bowl after defeating opponent Charles Harris *(right)* at the 1935 Spring Lake Invitational.

Frank Shields *(left)* and Frank Parker *(right)*.

The 1939 Seabright Tennis Club Invitational was one of seven men's singles titles Frank won in 1939.

Photo: Wide World Photos, Inc.

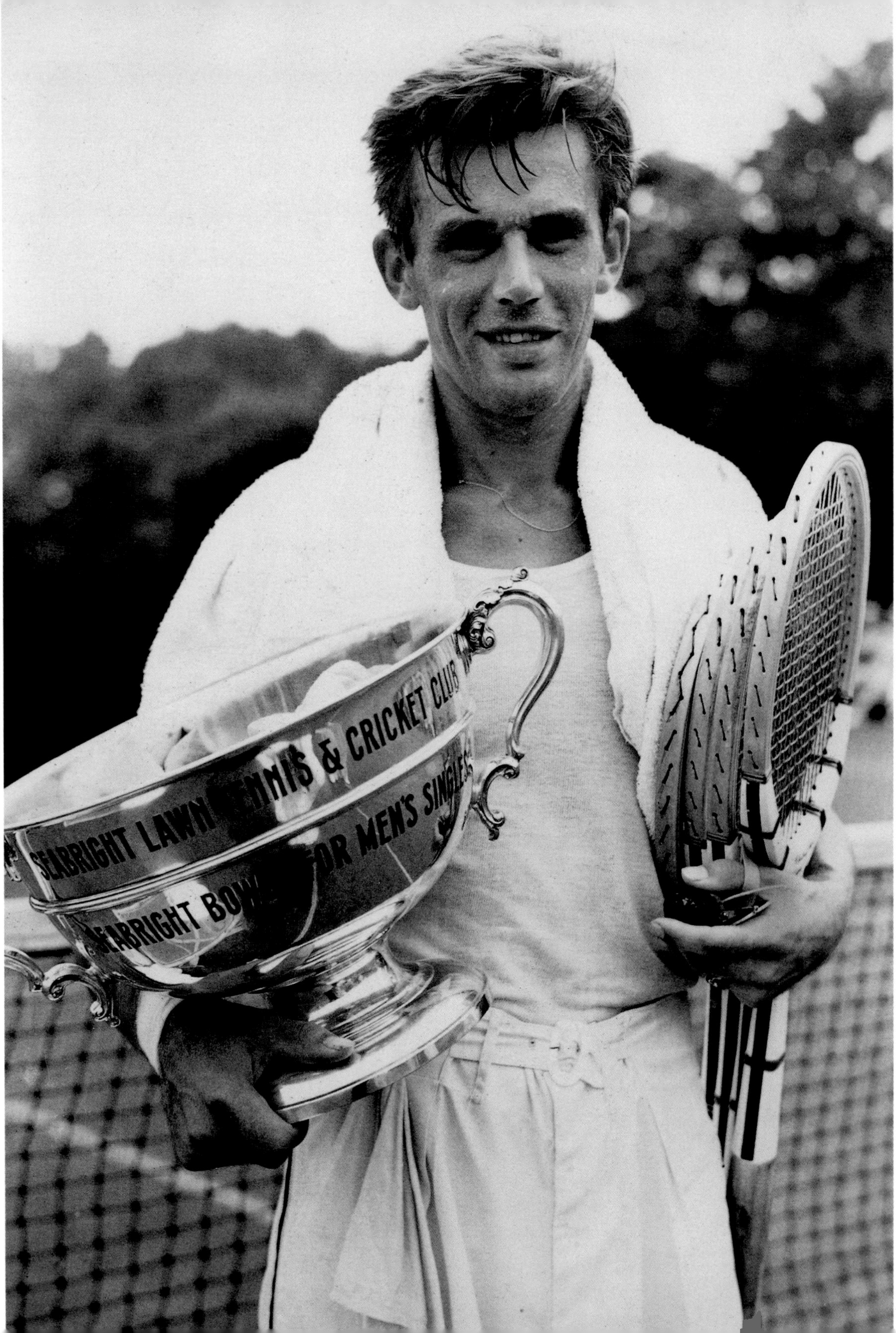

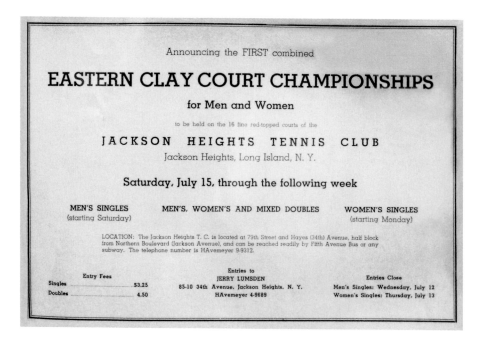

Announcing the FIRST combined

EASTERN CLAY COURT CHAMPIONSHIPS

for Men and Women

to be held on the 16 fine red-topped courts of the

JACKSON HEIGHTS TENNIS CLUB

Jackson Heights, Long Island, N. Y.

Saturday, July 15, through the following week

MEN'S SINGLES (starting Saturday)	MEN'S, WOMEN'S AND MIXED DOUBLES	WOMEN'S SINGLES (starting Monday)

LOCATION: The Jackson Heights T. C. is located at 79th Street and Hayes (34th) Avenue, half block from Northern Boulevard (Jackson Avenue), and can be reached readily by Fifth Avenue Bus or any subway. The telephone number is HAvemeyer 9-9312.

Entry Fees	Entries to JERRY LUMSDEN 85-10 34th Avenue, Jackson Heights, N. Y. HAvemeyer 4-9689	Entries Close
Singles _____ $3.25		Men's Singles: Wednesday, July 12
Doubles _____ 4.50		Women's Singles: Thursday, July 13

His success on the clay courts was phenomenal, and his timing and quickness were vital to his success. Gardnar Mulloy recalled, "Mr. Parker could play on any type of court. Even though he won the U.S. Nationals on grass at Forest Hills twice, his best surface was clay. Frank's steadiness destroyed everybody, and his uncanny backhand was a thing of beauty. It could be considered the best in the game with perhaps the exception of Don Budge's, which was a bit more powerful." Frank also excelled on grass at Seabright, Meadow Club, and the Eastern Grass Championships.

As Spring Lake and the U.S. Clay Court Championships were exceptional tournaments for Frank, 1937 was an exceptional year for Parker victories. He won the U.S. Indoor Championships men's singles and the men's doubles with Greg Mangin, and the Bermuda Lawn Tennis Club Championships men's singles and the men's doubles with Wayne Sabin, the Sugar Bowl Invitational in New Orleans, and the Seigniory Club International Championships in Quebec, as well as being selected for the Davis Cup Team for the first time.

However, 1937 also marked an event in Frank's life that caused a scandal which would forever overshadow his tennis performance. While Frank and the Beasleys were on a practice trip in Bermuda, Frank and Audrey Beasley confessed to Mercer that they had been in love for several years. After twenty-three years of marriage, the Beasleys separated. Several months later Audrey filed for divorce, and soon thereafter on March 17, 1938 in a Reno, Nevada, court house, Frank and Katherine (Audrey) Browne Beasley were wed. They honeymooned later that year during a stopover for a tennis exhibition in Cuba.

"Mercer Beasley, veteran tennis coach who lost a 'love match' to his onetime 'boy wonder' protégé, Frankie Parker, gave his blessing Saturday to the 22 year-old Davis cup star, now honeymooning in California [later honeymooning in Cuba] with Beasley's former wife. Beasley told all about the romance which he said he discovered 'in my own house' in Bermuda last year," reported the *Milwaukee Journal*. "The Beasley's children were Katherine, 21 and Jimmy, 14."

Newlyweds Audrey and Frank Parker honeymooned in Cuba during a stopover for a tennis exhibition in 1938.

The article continued, "Although both Frank and Mrs. Beasley gave their ages as 'over 21,' Mrs. Beasley is 42 or 43 and is described by friends as 'very attractive.' She charged extreme cruelty in her suit for divorce from the tennis professional." The newspaper explained Frank's attraction to Audrey, "Although Beasley taught him the fine points of tennis, it was Mrs. Beasley who managed his training, watched his diet, and in general exercised a mother's care."[23]

Because the Catholic Church did not approve of marriage to a divorced person, Frank did not phone his devoutly religious family with the news. They instead learned of the marriage when it was announced on a local Milwaukee radio station. Anna Paikowski was shocked. The family had known that the Beasleys were separated, but were not aware of Audrey and Frank's romantic relationship. The USLTA also frowned on the marriage by dropping Frank's national ranking from third to eighth place.

Frank and Audrey were often compared to the Duke and Duchess (also a divorcee) of Windsor, who got married in 1937 under considerable controversy. Many believed that Frank and Audrey's marriage would not last. However, they had a unique and inseparable relationship.

The Parkers eventually developed a wonderful friendship with Audrey. Mercer Beasley continued to attend Frank's matches, as a friend but not a coach. Frank, no longer under the strict regulations of Beasley's coaching, began to show a slice of personality.

"Parker is doing the best to live down his reputation as the 'mechanical man' of tennis," reported the *Milwaukee Journal.* "He is more colorful, his onetime poker face blossoms out with a smile every now and then, and a pair of dark glasses he wears to correct a slight case of nearsightedness gives him a more lively appearance on the courts. Players call him 'Mr. Incognito' because of the dark glasses and he appears to like it."[24]

After their honeymoon, Frank and Audrey moved to Beverly Hills, California. Here Frank found an exciting off-season career working for Metro-

Photo © Hulton-Deutsch Collection/Corbis.

Frank's signature dark glasses earned him the nickname "Mr. Incognito."

Though Audrey and
Frank's marriage was very
controversial, the couple
shared a unique and
inseparable relationship.

Working at MGM as
assistant director for
special effects afforded
Frank *(back row, fourth
from left)* many special
opportunities, such as
an invitation to actor
Lionel Barrymore's
(seated) birthday party.

Goldwyn-Mayer. He soon became friends with actor Gary Cooper and studio art director Cedric Gibbons, designer of the Oscar statue, who together helped Frank advance at MGM. He began as a bicycle messenger and rose to assistant director of special effects.

As assistant director Frank was extremely busy. He sometimes assisted with as many as twelve pictures at one time. For each picture he read the script and then helped develop the required special effects. In all he worked on approximately fifty movie sets, including *Mrs. Miniver*. He and Audrey were able to attend many exclusive MGM previews.

Convinced that Frank would make a great cowboy, Gary Cooper arranged an interview for him with Sam Goldwyn. Frank realized that tennis meant more to him than a possibly promising acting career, so he turned down the opportunity. Years later, however, he wondered often what his career as a full-time actor might have been like. Regardless of his own intentions to act or play tennis, his fate was cast in 1941 when he was drafted into the army.

In his position at MGM Frank was able to take Audrey to numerous movie screenings.

Photo: The Greegan Studios

Chapter Four

T H E

W A R

Y E A R S

Frank embarked on yet another path of adventure in the service.

During his two-month training at March Field in California, Frank organized tennis and badminton matches among his fellow servicemen. He was then transferred to Muroc Air Field Base in California, where he served in Special Services. His duties included driving to Los Angeles to pick up Bob Hope, Jimmy Durante, Jack Benny, and Bing Crosby to perform their radio shows at the air base.

During his stay at Muroc, Frank often hitchhiked home at 6:30 AM to stay with Audrey during two-day leaves. (And, if the opportunity arose, he played tennis at the Los Angeles Tennis Club.) He and Audrey wrote letters to each other nearly everyday. In one correspondence, Audrey informed Frank of a miscarriage. Though she had had two other children with Mercer, Audrey was deeply saddened. She eagerly awaited her husband's return.

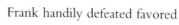

World War II found many tennis players enlisted in the service. Exhibition matches were held among the players to boost the morale of servicemen and raise money for the Red Cross. Because Frank's duties included serving as a calisthenics director and physical education officer to fellow servicemen, he was able to stay in top physical and mental shape and perform well in the exhibitions. He was also able to continue competing in amateur tournaments.

Frank handily defeated favored California natives Jack Kramer and Ted Schroeder in the Southern California Championships in May 1941. In July he won the U.S. Clay Court Championships in River Forest, Illinois. Journalist Jack Miller reported, "On Frank

Exhibition matches
boosted morale
and raised money
for the Red Cross.

Left: Frank and Bill
Tilden at March Field.

Below: Pancho Segura
and Frank.

Opposite page: **During
his duty in Special
Services at Muroc Air
Field Base, Frank
chauffeured perform-
ers, such as comedians
Bob Hope and Jerry
Colonna (*third and
fourth from left*), who
broadcast their radio
shows from the base.**

Andrew Parker's bronzed brow rests a rare honor, his third national clay court men's singles crown. By defeating Bitsy Grant, Don McNeill, and Bobby Riggs in the closing rounds the erstwhile schoolboy wonder entered that select little circle of players who have won the title three times or more. The list includes Bill Tilden (seven), Grant (three) and Riggs (three). Parker's previous victories were in 1933 and 1939."[25] Weeks later Frank went on to win the Eastern Clay Court Championships without losing a set, prompting *American Lawn Tennis* to refer to him as "the cynosure of all tennis eyes."[26]

In the third highest title in tennis, the Pacific Southwest Championships title, Frank was victorious in 1941 and 1942. He also excelled in doubles at the tournament, winning with Gene Mako in 1941 and Jack Kramer in 1943.

In September 1942 Frank traveled from Muroc Field to New York to participate in his country's most prestigious tournament, the U.S. Nationals at Forest Hills. (By 1944 half the contenders in the event were servicemen.) The trip was approved due to Frank's high ranking on the tennis circuit (No. 2). Having competed in the event every year since 1932, Frank finally made it to the final round but was defeated by Ted Schroeder (8-6, 7-5, 3-6, 4-6, 6-2). The opponent recalled, "I attacked Frank's backhand. Frank's forehand was so bad. On a crucial shot, Frank did not know where he was going to hit it. It was a matter of execution. On Frank's forehand, you did not know where it was going to go. On his backhand, you knew where it was going to go. The ability to force Frank to hit so many passing shots, and finally errors, would overtake him. You can beat a good player at the net."

Radio announcer Bill Stern summed up feelings over Frank's loss—

"...as Frank Parker reached the peak of his tennis game about seven years ago America was just forgetting the very colorful Bill Tilden, and America was just enjoying the very colorful Ellsworth Vines and Fred Perry—and America was just beginning to appreciate the very colorful Don Budge. These were all great tennis players, and who had time to look at an obscure tennis player named Frank Parker? But Frank wasn't dis-

Because of Frank's high ranking on the tennis circuit he was allowed temporary leave from the service to participate in the U.S. Nationals, the country's most prestigious tennis tournament. (*American Lawn Tennis*, August 5, 1942, 19)

couraged. He continued to play the best tennis he knew how—overshadowed by the brilliance of Don Budge.

And then Don Budge turned professional, and now, finally, Frank Parker was to have his day. But then, out of nowhere, three years ago, the year that Budge turned professional, another California youngster named Bobby Riggs hit the tennis spotlight, and the public that had just begun to know Frank Parker forgot him as they clamored for the new champion—the colorful Bobby Riggs. Still Frank plodded on—just another good tennis player with no color.

Last year Bobby Riggs started to slip and everybody said, "Well, now at last the public will get to know Frank Parker," but then out of nowhere came the prize screwball of all times to attract the tennis fans' attention. His name was Frankie Kovacs, and he wrote his name in large headlines because he could eat tennis balls and chew a tennis racket. Again Frank Parker was forgotten . . .

. . . But somewhere deep in the back of Frank Parker's mind he must have remembered the eight long years he had been trying for recognition, and he must have determined to come back and have one more fling at it. And so he came across the country this year to play in the National Tennis Championships.

. . . and I think as Frank Parker walked on the court yesterday afternoon he must have thought back to other Californians he had been up against in years gone by: Tilden, Budge, Riggs, Kovacs . . .

. . . and another Californian stood in his path. A youngster name Ted Schroeder. Schroeder won the first two sets yesterday afternoon, and he needed only one set to win the championship. Frank Parker looked for all the world like the Frank Parker who had figured in so many important matches. And even though the gallery conceded the victory to Schroeder, and even though Schroeder led two sets to love, Frank Parker demonstrated yesterday afternoon that he was not through. He won the the third set, and then he won the fourth set, and now at long last Frank Parker stood on the brink of the greatest championship in tennis. One more set and it would be all over, and he would have that title that had so long been denied him.

This was perhaps to be his last set of tennis in big time competition, for he was *old as tennis players go and that great fighting heart of his must have realized that the next few minutes were to make up for the eight years of heartache he had suffered.*

I would like to end this editorial tonight by saying that Frank Parker won that fifth set, and that at last he gained the recognition that was denied him for so long...but he didn't win. He lost that fifth set... lost it going down fighting... lost it as he had lost other matches in the past thirteen years... and today all America is hailing the new champion, Ted Schroeder.

But I would like to pay tribute tonight to the man who lost...to a man who in my humble opinion has the greatest fighting heart I have ever seen in sports...to a man, who even though he lost the championship, will always be a champion in my book!"

Jack Kramer and Frank were victorious in the men's doubles at the 1943 U.S. Nationals in which they defeated Bill Talbert and David Freeman (6-2, 6-4, 6-4), but the singles title still evaded him as he lost to Joe Hunt in the third round (3-6, 6-2, 6-3). In June 1944 Frank paired with Bill Canning in the Pacific Coast Doubles Championships at La Jolla Beach and Tennis Club to defeat Robert Kimbrell and Jack Knemeyer (6-2, 6-1, 6-1).

In September of 1944 Frank once again traveled to Forest Hills to participate in the U.S. Nationals. His confidence grew in the early rounds with wins over Bruce Thomas (6-0, 6-2), Vic Seixas (6-1, 6-4), Charles Oliver (6-2, 6-4, 6-1), and No. 2 seed Don McNeill (6-4, 3-6, 6-2, 6-2). Though Bill Talbert had beaten Pancho Segura in five sets in the semi-finals, Frank went on to beat Talbert (6-4, 3-6, 6-3, 6-3) and finally win the tournament. It was a major victory for Frank and his first grand slam* singles title. Mercer Beasley was at the finals to congratulate him.

"The boy wonder of lawn tennis may sometimes have felt lonely during the 13 years since he won the National Boy's Championship [U.S. Boys' Championships] at 15. He kept on playing year after year, breezed through the early rounds and then, with the goal in sight, was turned back on the thresh-

---

* One of the four major singles titles: the U.S. Nationals, Australian Championships, French Championships and Wimbledon.

old. Perseverance is alone an admirable quality. When it is joined to skill of execution and a canny brain, it is bound to win through in the end. So, those of us who believed in Parker during the years when the majority looked on him as just a good mechanical player without the touch of genius, rejoice that his years of patient perseverance have at last been rewarded by his win of the National Championship [U.S. Nationals] on Sept. 4th," reported journalist Edward C. Potter Jr.[27]

In 1945 Frank and Don Budge were stationed in Guam, where they joined Bobby Riggs and Wayne Sabin touring the Pacific Islands to play exhibition matches for their fellow servicemen. Frank fondly recalled the soldiers whistling at the players as they took to the tennis courts in their shorts.

Frank was now ranked No.1 by the USLTA. In September his commanding general ordered him to make the 9,000 mile flight to the U.S. to compete in the U.S. Nationals. Frank hoped to repeat his victory of 1944. He never lost a set, defeating George Ball (6-1, 6-2), Rolor Ray (6-1, 6-0), Sey-

Colonel Gerald Hoyle of Muroc Air Field Base congratulates Sgt. Frank Parker on his men's singles victory at the 1944 U.S. Nationals.

Photo: U.S. Army Air Forces

Frank and Don Budge
(back court, left to right)
play Bobby Riggs and
Wayne Sabin *(front court,
left to right)* on a tour of
the Pacific Islands to play
exhibition matches for
their fellow servicemen.

mour Greenburg (6-2, 6-3, 6-2), and Elwood Cooke (6-4, 8-6, 7-5). Frank once again faced Bill Talbert in the finals. And Talbert once again saw defeat (14-12, 6-1, 6-2). Frank had already devoured Talbert's game after the first set, which lasted over an hour. Talbert had injured his ankle the day before in the final point of the match, making it painful to run. Although Talbert's injury may have weakened his ability, Frank played a near-perfect game in the last two sets, hitting mostly from the backcourt. Talbert admitted, "The first set was close, but the rest was history."

World War II ended one day before the finals on September 2, 1945. Frank returned home to Audrey in Los Angeles.

Lt. Don Budge, Sgt. Frank Parker, and Lt. Harold Fenerty enjoy a moment of "levity" at Pearl Harbor in 1945.

Chapter Five

THE

DAVIS

CUP

One of the most celebrated achievements for amateur players of Frank's era was to be selected for the Davis Cup. The tournament, begun in 1900, is an international competition among four-player teams representing each competing country. The Davis Cup meant everything to Frank. He loved the tournament and was honored to have been chosen for the team.

The tryouts were extremely difficult in that era. Despite only a handful of top tennis players, they were all experts at the game. Frank succeeded in making the team in 1937, 1939, 1946, and 1948, with a record of 12-2. (The Davis Cup was not played from 1940–45 because of World War II.)

In 1937 the Davis Cup Team consisted of Frank, 21, Don Budge, 22, Gene Mako, 21, and Bitsy Grant, 27—the youngest team America had ever chosen. Walter Pate was the non-playing captain. Gene Mako recalled, "All of us were close friends, and Walter Pate was an ideal captain." The U.S. played Japan in the first round in San Francisco. Frank had two victories defeating J. Yamagishi (6-3, 2-6, 8-6, 6-1) and F. Nakano (6-0, 6-3, 6-2). During the July Challenge Round (the final round) at Wimbledon, England, Frank lost to Bunny Austin (6-3, 6-2, 7-5), but won the final match beating Charles Hare (6-2, 6-4, 6-2).

"Parker's crushing victory over Hare was a great surprise. Frankie went into the match the underdog. But Parker fulfilled all the predictions that were made of him when he was a 'schoolboy wonder' in 1930. He attacked with savage relentlessness and Hare never had a chance," wrote the *Milwaukee Journal*. "Parker was well-nigh perfect. Even his forehand, long a weak chink in his armor, was a thing of beauty. Shots made off that side had power and perfect length and accuracy. He was so good that Hare appeared as a third-rater throughout the match. The American fortified his perfect shots by faultless strategy and keen anticipation…The only thing Parker was willing to say about the match itself was that Hare 'Didn't play very well.' He possibly was the most modest Davis Cup hero on record."

Walter Pate said he never saw more perfect tennis, and young Frank said, "I'll never win one that will mean as much to me as that one." His victory helped the U.S. beat Great Britain 4-1 and brought the Davis Cup home after a ten-year absence.[28]

"Budge, Mako, Grant, Parker and Wayne Sabin returned with Captain Pate on the Manhattan. These boys, having accomplished something that no other American tennis players have been able to do for many years, might have been excused for celebrating a bit, even more than a little. But it seems that they use their court manners for everyday purposes, and their quiet behavior aboard ship was altogether admirable," wrote reporter Walter Schleiter.[29]

As a twenty-one-year-old Frank had impressions of England that included more than the prestige of being part of the Davis Cup. In a *Milwaukee Journal* article Frank stated, "They've [the British attendees] got to have their tea at 4 o'clock. The spectators spread cloths over their laps and had their tiffin right in the stands at Wimbledon." The young champion was also intrigued by the formalities required by the appearance of the king and queen. The players bowed from their waist, and the audience rose to their feet. Frank found it amusing that each time the queen stood to adjust her seat, the crowd all stood thinking she was getting up to leave.[30]

Wimbledon also afforded Frank the opportunity to become acquainted with two famous clothing designers. During the Davis Cup matches, the players were given complimentary tickets to all the games. A. J. Izod, president of Dozi clothing company, offered the players Dozi shirts, shorts, and sweaters in exchange for their tickets. Frank also became friends with René Lacoste, who had his own clothing line and was a well-known French tennis player and Davis Cup team member.

In 1939 Frank was selected for the Davis Cup team for a second time. The team consisted of Frank, Bobby Riggs, Joe Hunt, and Jack Kramer. In the Challenge Round held at Haverford, Pennsylvania, the U.S. played Australia. Frank and Riggs played singles. Hunt and Kramer played doubles. Frank

The 1939 Davis Cup
Team: Joe Hunt,
Frank Parker, Bobby
Riggs, and Tom Brown
with Audrey Parker
and Kay Riggs.

The 1946 U.S. Davis Cup
team, arriving at San Francisco
Airport on November 11, 1946:
(from back row, left to right)
Jack Kramer, Walter Pate, Tom
Brown, Gardnar Mulloy, Ted
Schroeder, Bill Talbert, and
Frank, accompanied by Audrey.

The 1946 U.S. Davis Cup
team: Gardnar Mulloy,
Bill Talbert, Walter Pate
(captain), Frank Parker,
Jack Kramer.

played two matches, beating Adrian Quist (6-3, 2-6, 6-4, 1-6, 7-5) and losing to John Bromwich (6-0, 6-3, 6-1). The U.S. team lost to Australia 3-2.

Following World War II, the Davis Cup returned to its normal schedule. Frank was chosen for the 1946 team, along with Ted Schroeder, Bill Talbert, Tom Brown, Jack Kramer, and Gardnar Mulloy. The first round was played in St. Louis. Frank beat F. H. Ampon (6-0, 6-0, 6-0) and A. J. Sanchez (6-1, 6-4, 6-0) to help the U.S. beat the Philippines 5-0. The North American zone final round was held at the Orange Lawn Tennis Club in New Jersey. Frank beat R. Vega (6-0, 6-0, 6-2) and A. Vega (6-3, 6-3, 6-2) to help the U.S. defeat Mexico 5-0. The inter-zone round was held in New York. Frank beat L. Bergelin (6-0, 3-6, 6-1, 6-1) and T. Johansson (9-7, 6-2, 6-1)to aid the U.S. victory over Sweden 5-0. The Challenge Round was held in December in Melbourne, Australia. Frank did not participate in any of the matches.

His absence from the Melbourne Challenge Round created quite a controversy reported by many Australian and U.S. newspapers. Frank felt team captain Walter Pate had passed him up unfairly in choosing Ted Schroeder, Jack Kramer, and Gardnar Mulloy for the singles matches. Frank was ranked No. 2, exceeded only by first-ranked Jack Kramer. Frank had won the U.S. Nationals in 1944 and 1945. He had won the preliminary games 6-0 and had beaten Ted Schroeder in the pre-trial matches. Frank beat No. 2-ranked Australian Dinny Pails in ten exhibition matches and John Bromwich of Australia in an exhibition match earlier that year. It appeared that because John Bromwich would be competing in the singles play, Frank's 1939 Davis Cup loss to Bromwich, though seven years earlier, was being held against him.

Bill Talbert felt that he, Frank, and Tom Brown, who also did not play any Challenge Round matches, were passed up because Perry Jones, president of the Southern California Tennis Association, had a specific interest in promoting Californians Kramer and Schroeder in the Davis Cup for future tennis exhibitions and had made a deal with Pate.

Team member Ted Schroeder had a different view, "It was simple. Pate called a meeting. He announced that Jack [Kramer] and I would play the singles. Pate adjourned the meeting for twenty-four hours. Then Pate decided that the players should choose the team. The six players cast their votes. Frank and Mulloy voted for themselves. Kramer, Brown, Talbert, and I voted for me (4-1-1)."

The choice of players for doubles competition was equally questionable. Kramer and Schroeder were chosen for the doubles match even though Mulloy and Talbert were the national doubles champions in 1945 and 1946, and Frank and Mulloy beat Kramer and Schroeder in the practice matches.

Despite the controversy over choice of players, the U.S. team had a 5-0 victory over Australia and brought the Davis Cup back to the United States. Ted Schroeder, who had played as an amateur on the tennis circuit from 1939–41, never turned professional. He had a full-time job and competed in tennis only when he had the time.

Walter Pate may have been unfair in not allowing Frank to play but did allow him to bring Audrey to Australia. Though Pate never let wives travel with the team, he made an exception for Audrey because of her

Photo: *The Herald*, Melbourne, Australia

positive affect on her husband's game. Frank often credited Audrey for his champion status.[31] She assisted him with everything from training to sewing his tennis shorts—complete with monogram. She encouraged Frank to practice deep shots to both corners of the tennis court. She made him sprint up and down the court stating, "To keep his muscles loose and flexible, Frank must be trained like a ballet dancer." She kept him on a strict rest schedule, avoiding numerous social functions during the trials.[32]

Though Frank was upset about the games, he and Audrey had a won-
derful time touring Australia. In temperatures over 100 degrees, Frank and
Audrey enjoyed the wildlife, the countryside, the zoo, and the horse races.
(Some of the horses were named after the American Davis Cup team players.)
Their visits to the hospitals and chats with the locals endeared them to the
Australian people.

When Frank arrived in Sydney, his bow tie, green-tinted glasses, and
Hollywood-like appearance enamored reporters, who thought he bore a strik-
ing resemblance to Frank Sinatra. They were equally entranced by Audrey,
reporting on the stylish hat, gloves, handbag, dress, or suit she wore to the
tennis tournaments.

In 1948 Frank was chosen for the Davis Cup team for the last time.
His teammates were Ted Schroeder, Gardnar Mulloy, and Bill Talbert. Frank
won two matches in the Challenge Round held at Forest Hills, defeating
Australians Bill Sidwell (6-4, 6-4, 6-4) and Adrian Quist (6-2, 6-2, 6-3). The
American team beat Australia 5-0.

In later life Frank lamented the lost luster of the Davis Cup, "Today
the players decide whether they want to play or not. They make more money
playing exhibitions, so the Davis Cup has suffered."

POST-WAR

SUCCESS

Two weeks after the war ended, Frank competed at the Pacific Southwest Championships in Los Angeles. He reigned once again in singles, defeating Herbert Flam (6-2, 6-4) and in doubles with Frank Shields, defeating Pancho Segura and Bill Talbert (6-4, 6-2). Frank repeated his doubles' victories in the tournament in 1947 and 1948.

In October of 1945 Frank traveled to Mexico to earn titles in the Pan-American Championships singles and doubles tournaments. As is often the case in tennis, Frank and Pancho Segura not only rose to the top in winning the doubles championship but found themselves competing against each other in the finals of the singles tournament. Segura said recently he felt lucky he was able to play with Frank as an amateur and professional, "Frank was a role model of that era. He did not smoke, drink, or chase girls. After all, Frank ended the chase when he met Audrey. Frank beat everyone. He was one of the great players. He was always a pleasure to be around, always an inspiration, and had a great temperament. His backhand was the finest with great control."

When compared to the athleticism of Pancho Segura, Frank's method of play, often criticized as lacking color, had some tennis fans questioning his skill, but writer Gasper Octavio Almanza defended Frank's competence, "The amount of muscular effort displayed by the South American in reaching some balls border on the incredible and are, surely, beyond the ability of many a tournament player. Such lavish expenditure of energy, which crowds take for fighting spirit, delights the galleries beyond measure and stirs them to a frenzy.

Because dunces do not see Parker resort to squirrel-like bustle they pronounce him slow of foot. They do not stop to consider how many of Segura's drop-shots that would have scored against anybody else, were easily reached by Parker and turned into earned points. This should certainly prove great foot-speed and something worth a lot more: mental alertness and gift of anticipation."[33]

As U.S. Ambassador of Sports, Frank was able to compete internationally and travel extensively with Audrey.

Photo: London News Agency

Buenos Aires Zoo — November 19, 1947 —

61

Frank experienced another year of success in 1946 with one doubles and five singles victories. His win at the Eastern Clay Court Championships in July gave him permanent possession of the Jackson Heights challenge trophy, having previously won in 1940 and 1941. The event was also memorable in that it was the first televised Eastern Clay Court Championship. The uniqueness of the television cameras "wooed many of the spectators away from the matches inside the gate," noted *American Lawn Tennis*.[34]

In 1947 Frank not only matched his number of singles victories of the previous year, but demonstrated his skill at doubles play by winning nine doubles titles—five with Gardnar Mulloy, three with Pancho Segura, and one with Jaroslav Drobny. He also made it to the final round of the U.S. Nationals for the fourth time in his career, but lost to Jack Kramer (4-6, 2-6, 6-1, 6-0, 6-3).

In May 1948 the USLTA chose Frank as the U.S. Ambassador of Sports, an expense-paid sponsorship to play in various tournaments. In years past Frank had been unable to play in the French Championships or Wimbledon due to lack of funds for traveling. The ambassadorship enabled him to travel and compete all over Europe. He visited Belgium, England, France, Scandinavia, Spain, and Switzerland. He was also received by Pope Pius XII at the Vatican, King Frederik IX in Denmark, King Gustav V in Sweden, King Haakon VII in Norway, and the royal family in Egypt. He not only took in the sights but grabbed every title within his grasp.

During his first year of travels abroad Frank won the ultimate clay court challenge—the French Championships (currently the French Open) at Stade Roland Garros Stadium in Paris. On his way to the finals Frank defeated Peter Hare of England (6-1, 6-1, 6-1), Bernard Destremau of France (8-6, 4-6, 7-5, 13-11), Gianni Cucelli of Italy (6-1, 6-2, 6-1), and Eric Sturgess of South Africa (6-2, 6-2, 6-1). In the finals he defeated Jaroslav Drobny of Czechoslovakia (6-4, 7-5, 5-7, 8-6). Frank won the French Crown (the trophy of the French Championships) on his first attempt, a feat also accomplished by fellow

American Lawn Tennis

The Illustrated Magazine of the Game

Frank's performance at the 1947 U.S. Nationals earned him the cover of *American Lawn Tennis*, but not the title.

FOUNDED IN 1907 BY
S. WALLIS MERRIHEW

**Kramer won the title—
Parker won the crowd**

OCTOBER, 1947
50 CENTS

As U.S. Ambassador of Sports, Frank had the opportunity to meet the nobility of the countries he visited, such as King Frederik IX of Denmark *(top)*, King Gustav V of Sweden *(left)*, and King Haakon VII of Norway *(below)*.

Photo: G. Felici/Rome

While visiting the
Vatican, Audrey and
Frank were also re-
ceived by Pope Pius XII.

In 1949 the Mexican government commissioned famed artist Diego Rivera *(left)* to paint a portrait of Audrey and Frank. In 1990 Frank sold the portrait *(below)* for $120,000.

Americans Don Budge and Don McNeill. In that year Frank also won the Belgian Championships men's singles defeating Budge Patty (6-1, 1-6, 3-6, 6-1, 6-2) and joined forces with Patty to win the men's doubles title.

As the European tennis season came to an end, Frank moved on to the Pan-American Championships in Mexico City, where he and doubles partner Pancho Gonzales defeated Jaroslav Drobny and Eric Sturgess (7-9, 6-2, 8-6, 6-2). The Mexican government, enchanted by Frank, commissioned world-renowned artist Diego Rivera to paint a portrait of the Parkers. Frank waived his appearance fee for the tournament in exchange for the portrait. Though Frank and Audrey sat for Rivera two hours a day for a week, Frank thoroughly enjoyed the experience and described Rivera as "good humored and overweight." Frank eventually sold the valuable painting in November 1990 through Sotheby's in New York for approximately $120,000.

The year 1949 began with a string of continuous wins in Europe for Frank, impressing sportswriters and fans with his seemingly flawless execution. In February he became the first American to win the men's singles French Indoor Championships. He defeated Scandinavian Kurt Nielsen in the quarterfinals (10-8, 6-4, 2-6, 6-2), Frenchman Henri Cochet in the semi-finals (6-2, 6-4, 9-7), and Frenchman Marcel Bernard in the finals (6-1, 4-6, 6-3, 6-2). Frank and Henri Cochet also defeated Marcel Bernard and Jean Borotra (6-4, 3-6, 6-3, 7-5, 6-4) to gain the men's doubles title.

Frank continued his travels south to play in the Egyptian Championships in Cairo and the Egyptian International Championships in Alexandria two weeks later. Though dysentery caused Frank to lose eight pounds and become very weak, he still managed to win both the singles

With partner Pancho Gonzales (right), Frank won the men's doubles titles at the 1948 Pan-American Championships and the 1949 French Championships and Wimbledon.

and doubles events in both tournaments and take Audrey on a trip down the Nile. In Cairo he defeated Budge Patty in singles (6-2, 9-7, 8-6) and with Patty as his partner defeated Gottfried von Cramm and Jack Harper (5-7, 6-3, 7-5). In Alexandria he defeated Pedro Massip in singles (6-3, 6-2, 6-2) and with von Cramm as his partner defeated Patty and Harper (3-6, 6-2, 6-2, 5-7, 7-5).

His year of success continued in France in April when he won the Monte Carlo International Championships, defeating Gianni Cucelli of Italy (2-6, 6-3, 6-0, 6-4), and the singles title at the Paris Championships, defeating Marcel Bernard in the finals (6-0, 5-7, 3-6, 9-7, 6-2). In May he earned a fourth French title and executed another grand slam singles title by winning the French Championships (French Open) for the second time. He defeated Digutin Mitic in the quarterfinals (6-0, 6-2, 6-4), Eric Sturgess in

the semi-finals (6-2, 6-1, 6-4), and Budge Patty in the finals (6-3, 1-6, 6-1, 6-4). Frank is only one of three male Americans ever to win the French Open twice. (Tony Trabert did so with wins in 1954 and 1955, and Jim Courier won in 1991 and 1992.) Trabert commented on Frank's success, "Frank's record speaks for itself. He won the singles twice at the U.S. Nationals at Forest Hills on grass. He won the French Championships twice on clay. He was always a gentleman on and off the court. He was a true champion."

Frank earned another major title with his victory in the men's doubles French Championships with partner Pancho Gonzales, defeating Eustace Fannin and Eric Sturgess in the finals (6-3, 8-6, 5-7, 6-3). Frank excelled in doubles competition. He and Pancho Gonzales also won the men's doubles in Wimbledon defeating Gardnar Mulloy and Ted Schroeder in the finals (6-4, 6-4, 6-2).

As his stunning season of victories drew to a close Frank defeated Jaroslav Drobny (6-1, 2-6, 6-3, 6-4) in the eighth annual Pan-American Championships—the last amateur tournament of his career.

Frank was victorious in both the singles and doubles tournaments at the 1949 Egyptian Championships in Cairo and Egyptian International Championships in Alexandria. He celebrated by taking Audrey for a trip down the Nile.

Chapter Seven

TURNING

PRO

On October 17, 1949, eight days after his victory in Mexico City, Frank followed in the footsteps of Jack Kramer, Pancho Segura, and Pancho Gonzales and signed a professional contract with Bobby Riggs' tennis troupe earning $25,000 for a seven-month tour in 90 U.S. cities.[35] Though Audrey objected because a professional career would involve more frequent travel, and Frank was hesitant because of his recent success on the amateur circuit (1948 and 1949 were two of his best years) the couple's financial needs won out. Audrey's mother was ill. They needed the money for hospital bills and their own expenses.

Professional tennis appeared to agree with Frank. After the troupe's debut at Madison Square Garden, Alice Marble wrote, "Frank was quite, re-served—almost Sphinxlike—on the court as an amateur. To many fans, he was a dull performer. On opening night at the Garden, however, he was a different Parker, smiling and aggressive in his play. He generously rallied with a ball boy during the intermission and even went so far as to do a quiet little jig in time to the organ music. He seemed happy to be a professional."[36]

But despite being listed by *American Lawn Tennis* as among the top ten American tennis players in the first half of the century,[37] Frank's professional career lasted only two years. Pro tournaments were usually played on hard indoor courts. Frank was a master on clay and grass, but his performance suffered on the hard indoor surface.

He was able to earn additional money by agreeing to be a sponsor for the sporting goods manufacturer MacGregor, Inc. He promoted their tennis balls, rackets, and shirts from 1950 to 1952. Frank also took advantage of his charm and good looks by appearing in magazine ads for Chesterfield cigarettes and Milwaukee's Blatz beer.

After the war Frank had also returned to the sets of MGM to pursue the acting career that had tempted him earlier. Though he officially continued in his prior position as assistant director of special effects, the contacts he had made in the past playing tennis with movie stars proved advantageous. In 1951

As a professional player Frank was able to accept sponsorships, such as that for his hometown product Blatz Beer.

"I'm from Milwaukee, I ought to know...

Blatz is Milwaukee's Finest Beer!"

Says *Frank Parker* Star of the Bobby Riggs Tennis Troupe, appearing in over 100 U.S. Cities

"Yes, I was born and raised in Milwaukee," says Frank Parker. "So I know from experience that Milwaukeeans get their pick of the nation's best beers. And their first choice is Blatz. The reason is simple. Blatz is Milwaukee's *favorite* because it's Milwaukee's *finest* beer!" Yes—*official figures* show that Blatz is the *largest-selling beer in Milwaukee and all Wisconsin*, too. Try Blatz Beer, today!

Milwaukee is proud of Frank Parker's spectacular tennis record. He has twice been U.S. Champion, and has ranked among the top tennis ten for 16 years. Every year, Frank vacations at his parents' Milwaukee home.

"It's smart to serve Blatz!" says Frank Parker. Ask for Blatz at your favorite club, tavern, restaurant, package or neighborhood store. It's Milwaukee's *finest* beer.

Blatz

BETTER TASTING BEER FOR THE 99TH YEAR

Blatz is Milwaukee's First Bottled Beer!

TUNE IN DUFFY'S TAVERN Thursday Evening, 9:30 E.D.S.T., N.B.C.

© 1950, Blatz Brewing Co., Est. 1851 in Milwaukee, Wis.

Blatz Brewing Co.

Frank also accepted
a sponsorship with
MacGregor, Inc., a
leading tennis goods
manufacturer. (*American
Lawn Tennis*, April
1951, August 1, 1950
and February 1951.)

**As a MacGregor
sponsor Frank made
numerous appearances
to meet his fans.**

Kirk Douglas helped him land a role as a newspaperman in Paramount's *The Big Carnival*, a.k.a *Ace in the Hole*.

In March Frank also worked for 20th Century-Fox as an advisor for the film *Follow the Sun: The Ben Hogan Story*.[38] In 1952 MGM asked Frank to train Katherine Hepburn to play tennis for her role as Babe Didrikson Zaharias in the movie *Pat and Mike*. Hepburn was renting Cary Grant's home at the time. When Frank pulled into Grant's driveway, Hepburn stopped him and demanded proof that he was *the* Frank Parker. Frank eventually not only trained her to be a convincing tennis player in the film, but used his multiple talents to write the tennis scenes, work on the special effects, and play in the doubles matches with Hepburn, Gussy Moran, and Don Budge.

Frank's tennis skill and personality earned him many friends in Hollywood including Clark Gable, Errol Flynn, Van Johnson, William Powell, Robert Taylor, Gilbert Roland, Spencer Tracy, and Mickey Rooney. He golfed at Bel-Air Country Club with Bob Sterling, Fred MacMurray, Bob Wagner, Randolph Scott, and Hogie Carmichael and played tennis with Charlie Chaplin at Chaplin's home in Beverly Hills. Frank laughingly recalled, "We brought our own tennis balls to Charlie Chaplin's because Chaplin used to put his in the washing machine so he could reuse them."

Kirk Douglas helped Frank land a role as a newspaperman in the 1951 Paramount film *The Big Carnival*.

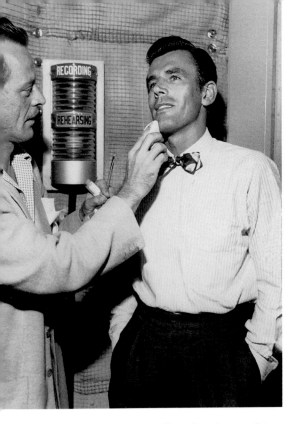

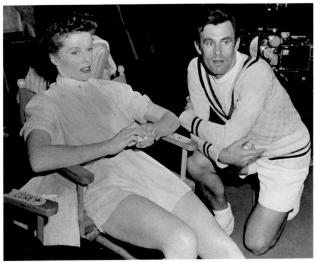

Photo: MGM

Photo: MGM

Above: A make-up artist prepares Frank for a scene in *The Big Carnival.*

Top right: Frank trained Katherine Hepburn to play tennis for her role as Babe Didrikson Zaharias in the 1952 film *Pat and Mike.*

Bottom right: Frank also appeared in the film playing a doubles match with *(left to right)* Katherine Hepburn, Gussie Moran, and Don Budge.

Chapter Eight

STILL

IN THE

LIMELIGHT

In the summer of 1952 Frank and Audrey decided to return to the Midwest. They purchased a home in Evanston, Illinois, and Frank took a job as a salesman with Hoerner Waldorf Corp., a corrugated box company, where he worked until 1976. During his twenty-four years of service at Hoerner, Frank received numerous awards as top salesman. Though his natural charm and wit helped him excel in sales, he also earned favor with many of his clients by "schmoozing" them on the tennis courts.

Frank also continued to participate in exhibitions and celebrity and benefit tournaments, such as the Symphony Tennis Classic in Minneapolis and the Alan King Tennis Classic at Caesar's Palace in Las Vegas. Being much older than Frank and having put on extra weight Audrey became increasingly uncomfortable with her young handsome husband playing mixed doubles and asked him not to do so. Throughout their years in Evanston Frank continued to enjoy the limelight, while Audrey preferred a more reclusive lifestyle.

In 1968 after eighteen years of retirement from the pro circuit Frank returned to Forest Hills to compete in his last professional tournament—one in which he had been victorious in 1943, 1944, and 1945—the U.S. Open, formerly the U.S. Nationals. Until that time the tournament was strictly open to amateur players, but a new ruling opened the field to professionals. So, at the age of fifty-two, Frank entered the tournament and became its oldest participant to this date. He lost in the second round to Arthur Ashe, who went on to win the title.

Frank and Audrey continued to live happily in Evanston until 1971, when Audrey passed away at the age of seventy-five due to heart trouble. Five years later one of Frank's very dear and close friends, Jerry Wexler, convinced him to move to the city. Wexler was a successful real estate developer who owned numerous buildings in Chicago, including the Drake Hotel. (The Drake's Cape Cod Room restaurant was one of Frank's favorite places to dine.) Wexler generously invited Frank to live "rent free" in a building he owned on McClurg Court in Chicago's Streeterville community. The high-

Frank's continued participation in celebrity events
and exhibitions gave him
the opportunity to meet
sports legends such as
Boston Red Sox outfielder
Ted Williams *(left)*, golf
champion Arnold Palmer
(right), heavyweight
champion Jack Dempsey
(below, center), and New
York Yankees outfielder
Joe DiMaggio *(below, right)*.

Photo: Bob Davidoff

rise apartment, two blocks west of Lake Michigan, offered a magnificent view of the city and lake. Frank's trophies and photographs soon covered the apartment's shelves and walls.

In the fall of 1976 Frank became emeritus director of tennis at the McClurg Court Sports Center. In his new position, Frank gave lessons and played tennis with members almost everyday. His game kept much of its edge as he continued to consistently ace his opponents. Frank's advice for young tennis players was, "Take lessons, learn the basics first, learn proper strokes, test the weight of the racket, have it strung correctly, and don't try to hit the ball too hard. And, have two sports in mind, because not everyone can make it as a tennis professional."

Frank also enjoyed playing weekly matches at the club with his friends. Though they tried their best to beat him, Frank never let up, even questioning many of their line calls.

Several of Hollywood's tennis aficionados, such as Bill Cosby, Dinah Shore, Burt Bacharach, Charleton Heston, Hugh O'Brien, Dustin Hoffman, and Barbara Eden, came to visit Frank for lessons or friendly competition. Former tennis competitors Pancho Gonzales, Don Budge, and Fred Perry also paid Frank many visits.

After eighteen years of Frank's dedicated service to the McClurg Court Sports Center, the club rewarded him by naming the tennis courts "The Frank Parker Tennis Center" in his honor.

Though Frank had long retired from the professional circuit, he continued to live the life of a celebrity. His sense of humor, good looks, and charming smile endeared him to all who crossed his path. "Happy" Rockefeller once recognized Frank in a hotel elevator in Hawaii and confessed with great enthusiasm that she had had a crush on him since watching him play in a tournament in Philadelphia years before. Singers Tony Bennett and Placido Domingo became good friends with Frank and always reserved a front row seat for him when performing in Chicago.

Photo: Mary Edsey

Frank Parker Tennis Center at the McClurg Court Sports Center in Chicago.

Photo: Archie Lieberman

Throughtout his career Frank was afforded the opportunity to meet many legendary figures, such as Charleton Heston *(top left)*, English tennis champion Fred Perry *(center left)*, singer Tony Bennett *(bottom left)*, and President John F. Kennedy *(below)*.

Bill Cosby met Frank on an elevator in a hotel in Pebble Beach, California. He saw the racket in Frank's hand and invited Frank to play tennis, not recognizing who he was. Frank stunned Cosby with his level of play and confessed he was a professional tennis player. Cosby, an avid player himself who participated in celebrity tournaments, eventually wrote a book on tennis and asked Frank to write the introduction.

Frank played tennis with Robert and Ethel Kennedy at their home in Palm Beach, Florida, and joined Mrs. Kennedy for the Dinah Shore Tennis Tournament, promoted by Alan King, in Las Vegas. Frank received many invitations from Mrs. Kennedy to attend parties in New York and had the honor of meeting President John F. Kennedy at a fundraiser in Chicago. In the 1970s he was invited to play in tennis exhibitions held for the Robert F. Kennedy Memorial.

From 1973 to 1979 Frank participated in the Grand Masters, a exhibition prize money tournament begun by Cincinnati businessman Al Bunis, which traveled throughout the U.S. featuring ex-champions over forty-five. In 1980 Frank refereed the Chicago Challenge of Champions Tennis Tournament in Chicago.

In addition to the many championships Frank had won, he received numerous honors after his professional tennis career had ended. He was inducted into the Wisconsin Hall of Fame in Milwaukee, Wisconsin, in 1960; the National Polish-American Sports Hall of Fame in Detroit, Michigan, in 1981; the Western Tennis Hall of Fame in Indianapolis, Indiana, in 1984; the Senior Hall of Fame in Minneapolis, Minnesota, in 1987; and the Lawrenceville Alumni Athletic Hall of Fame in 1996. In addition, Frank's best friend, Jack McGann, honored Frank with a "Wall of Fame" at his Evergreen Racquet and Fitness Club in Evergreen Park, Illinois. The display still showcases several of Frank's trophies and a wonderful display of photographs.

In 1966 Frank received the highest achievement of his career when he was inducted into the International Tennis Hall of Fame in Newport, Rhode

Plaque inducting Frank into the National Polish-American Sports Hall of Fame.

James Stewart, John Hennessey, George Lott, and Frank Parker being inducted into the Western Tennis Hall of Fame, August 11, 1984.

Island. Tennis great Eddie Moylan spoke of Frank's well-deserved induction, "He walks into the Hall of Fame with all the other great players. Comparing him to any present players, I really can't think of any of his style. He and Ken Rosewall had the beautiful classical style."

In 1987 Prince Rainier presented Frank with a trophy at the Monte Carlo International Championships. Ten years later Frank was invited to France to attend the anniversary of the tournament. Frank was also invited to join other past champions to sit with the royal family in the Royal Box at Wimbledon and the President's Box at the French Open in Stade Roland Garros Stadium. He received first class invitations to the U.S. Open and the Hall of Fame dinner at the Waldorf.

A Chance for Children Foundation honored Frank at the Chicago Hilton as "1991 Man of the Year." The event drew over 2,000 people and raised over $300,000. And in the summer of 1996 Frank was invited back to the Spring Lake Bath and Tennis Club for an entire weekend of events held in his honor.

Between the award functions of his later years, Frank spent his time attending charity benefits, reading novels, attending movies, and

Trophy case at Evergreen Racquet and Fitness Club in Evergreen Park, Illinois.

Photo: Mary Edsey

Hall of Fame dinner at the Waldorf Hotel in New York: *(standing, left to right)* Fred Stolle, Don Budge, Arthur Ashe, Tony Trabert, Jack Kramer, Vic Seixas, Pancho Segura, Manuel Santana, Neal Fraser, Stan Smith, Bill Talbert, Dick Savitt, Fred Perry, Frank Parker; *(seated, left to right)* Althea Gibson, Sara Palfrey Cooke, Pam Shriver, Virginia Wade, Pauline Betz Addie.

Portrait of "1991 Man
of the Year," Frank
Parker, by Carla
Beninati, awarded by
A Chance for Children
Foundation.

playing golf. He never remarried, but had a wonderful relationship with Janelle Robert, who resided in Jackson, Mississippi. On his sixty and seventieth birthdays, Frank was given elaborate and unforgettable birthday parties by Jerry and Sue Wexler.

In 1993 Frank survived a triple-bypass operation, but in 1997 the odds were finally against this legendary man—Frank was diagnosed with a blood clot in his lung. On the advise of his doctor, Frank traveled to San Diego Hospital for surgery to remove the clot. He characteristically maintained his cheery attitude—flirting with the nurses. But Frank Parker never recovered from the surgery. He passed away on July 24 at the age of eighty-one.

His million-dollar estate was endowed in thirds to his family members (which included a few nieces, nephews, and one brother-in-law), his former secretary at Hoerner Waldorf Corp., and his best friend, Jack McGann, who took care of him until his last day.

Life had been very good to Frank. He once said that if he had to do it again there would be absolutely nothing he would have changed about his life. "My work is play and vice versa," he said with that charming smile.

USLTA National Rankings for Frank Parker [*]

1933 – 8	1942 – 2
1934 – 4	1943 – 8
1935 – 7	1944 – 1
1936 – 2	1945 – 1
1937 – 3	1946 – 3
1938 – 8	1947 – 2
1939 – 2	1948 – 3
1940 – 5	1949 – 4
1941 – 3	

[*] Frank Parker's record of seventeen consecutive years in the USLTA's top ten was unsurpassed until 1988 when Jimmy Connors reached eighteen consecutive years, followed by nineteen in 1989. (Collins, Bud. *Bud Collins' Tennis Encyclopedia.* 3rd ed. Detroit, MI: Visible Ink Press, 1997.)

International Rankings for Frank Parker

1937 – 9

1938 (not ranked)

1939 – 5

1940-45 (not ranked)

1946 – 9

1947 – 3

1948 – 1

1949 – 5

(Brady, Maurice. *The Encyclopedia of Lawn Tennis.* London: Robert Hale Limited, 1958.)

Appendix

1930   **Western Boys' Championships** St. John's Military Academy; Delafield, Wisconsin

U.S. Boys' Championships Culver Military Academy; Culver, Indiana; doubles (partner, George Boynton)

1931   **U.S. Boys' Championships** Culver Military Academy; Culver, Indiana

1932   **Canadian Championships** Rideau Lawn Tennis Club; Ottawa, Ontario

U.S. Junior Championships Culver Military Academy; Culver, Indiana

1933   **River Oaks Country Club Invitational** Houston, Texas

U.S. Clay Court Championships Chicago Town and Tennis Club; Chicago, Illinois

Kentucky State Championships Louisville Boat Club; Louisville, Kentucky

Spring Lake Bathing and Tennis Club Invitational Spring Lake, New Jersey

1934   **Kentucky State Championships** Louisville Boat Club; Louisville, Kentucky

Spring Lake Bathing and Tennis Club Invitational Spring Lake, New Jersey; singles and doubles (partner, Johnny Van Ryn)

Seabright Tennis Club Invitational Seabright, New Jersey; doubles (partner, John Doeg)

Meadow Club Invitational Southampton, New York

Seigniory Club International Championships Lucerne, Quebec

1935   **Spring Lake Bathing and Tennis Club Invitational** Spring Lake, New Jersey; singles and doubles (partner, Gil Hall)

Seabright Tennis Club Invitational Seabright, New Jersey

Meadow Club Invitational Southampton, New York; singles and doubles (partner, Greg Mangin)

Newport Casino Lawn Tennis Club Invitational Newport, Rhode Island; doubles (partner, Frank Shields)

★All tournaments are singles matches unless otherwise noted.

Pennsylvania State Clay Court Championships Oakmont Tennis Club; Allentown, Pennsylvania

1936 **Wisconsin Open Championships** Milwaukee Town Club; Milwaukee, Wisconsin

Spring Lake Bathing and Tennis Club Invitational Spring Lake, New Jersey
Longwood Cricket Club Invitational Chestnut Hill, Massachusetts
Meadow Club Invitational Southampton, New York; singles and doubles (partner, Greg Mangin)

1937 **Sugar Bowl Invitational** New Orleans Country Club; New Orleans, Louisiana

U.S. Indoor Championships Seventh Regiment Armory; New York, New York; singles and doubles (partner, Greg Mangin)
Bermuda Lawn Tennis Club Championships Hamilton, Bermuda; singles and doubles (partner, Wayne Sabin)
Seigniory Club International Championships Lucerne, Quebec

1938 **Spring Lake Bathing and Tennis Club Invitational** Spring Lake, New Jersey; singles and doubles (partner, Wilmer Allison)

Canadian Championships Toronto Tennis Club; Toronto, Ontario; singles and doubles (partner, Wilmer Allison)

1939 **Southern California Championships** Los Angeles Tennis Club; Los Angeles, California

U.S. Clay Court Championships River Forest Tennis Club; River Forest, Illinois; singles and doubles (partner, Gene Mako)
Heart of America Championships Rockhill Tennis Club; Kansas City, Missouri
St. Louis Country Club Invitational St. Louis, Missouri; singles and doubles (partner, Gene Mako)
Spring Lake Bathing and Tennis Club Invitational Spring Lake, New Jersey; singles and doubles (partner, Gene Mako)

Kentucky State Championships Louisville Boat Club; Louisville, Kentucky

Seabright Tennis Club Invitational Seabright, New Jersey

Meadow Club Invitational Southampton, New York; double (partner, Don McNeill)

1940 **Heart of America Championships** Rockhill Tennis Club; Kansas City, Missouri

Spring Lake Bathing and Tennis Club Invitational Spring Lake, New Jersey

Eastern Clay Court Championships Jackson Heights Tennis Club; New York, New York

1941 **Pacific Coast Doubles Championships** Santa Barbara Biltmore Hotel; Santa Barbara, California (partner, Gene Mako)

Southern California Championships Los Angeles Tennis Club; Los Angeles, California

U.S. Clay Court Championships River Forest Tennis Club; River Forest, Illinois

Tri-State Championships Cincinnati Tennis Club; Cincinnati, Ohio; singles and doubles (partner, Gene Mako)

Eastern Clay Court Championships Jackson Heights Tennis Club; New York, New York

New York State Championships Seminole Tennis Club; Forest Hills, New York

Spring Lake Bathing and Tennis Club Invitational Spring Lake, New Jersey

Pacific Southwest Championships Los Angeles Tennis Club; Los Angeles, California; singles and doubles (partner, Gene Mako)

1942 **Pacific Southwest Championships** Los Angeles Tennis Club; Los Angeles, California

1943 **Longwood Cricket Club Invitational** Chestnut Hill, Massachusetts; doubles (partner, Jack Kramer)

U.S. Nationals West Side Tennis Club; Forest Hills, New York; doubles (partner, Jack Kramer)

Pacific Southwest Championships Los Angeles Tennis Club; Los Angeles, California; doubles (partner, Jack Kramer)

1944   **Pacific Coast Doubles Championships** La Jolla Beach and Tennis Club; La Jolla, California (partner, Bill Canning)

U.S. Nationals West Side Tennis Club; Forest Hills, New York

Pacific Southwest Championships Los Angeles Tennis Club; Los Angeles, California

1945   **La Jolla Beach and Tennis Club Invitational** La Jolla, California; singles and doubles (partner, John Sisson)

U.S. Nationals West Side Tennis Club; Forest Hills, New York

Pacific Southwest Championships Los Angeles Tennis Club; Los Angeles, California; singles and doubles (partner, Frank Shields)

Pan-American Championships Centro Deportivo Chapultepec; Mexico City, Mexico; singles and doubles (partner, Pancho Segura)

1946   **Heart of America Championships** Rockhill Tennis Club; Kansas City, Missouri

U.S. Clay Court Championships River Forest Tennis Club; River Forest, Illinois

Eastern Clay Court Championships Jackson Heights Tennis Club; New York, New York

Spring Lake Bathing and Tennis Club Invitational Spring Lake, New Jersey; singles and doubles (partner, Gardnar Mulloy)

Eastern Grass Court Championships Orange Lawn Tennis Club; South Orange, New Jersey; doubles (partner, Tom Brown)

1947   **Southern California Championships** Los Angeles Tennis Club; Los Angeles, California; doubles (partner, Pancho Segura)

Pacific Coast Doubles Championships La Jolla Beach and Tennis Club; La Jolla, California (partner, Pancho Segura)

Heart of America Championships Rockhill Tennis Club; Kansas City, Missouri; singles and doubles (partner, Gardnar Mulloy)

Southern Lawn Tennis Invitational New Orleans Tennis Club; New Orleans, Louisiana; singles and doubles (partner, Gardnar Mulloy)

U.S. Clay Court Championships Salt Lake Tennis Club; Salt Lake City, Utah

Eastern Clay Court Championships Jackson Heights Tennis Club; New York, New York

Spring Lake Bathing and Tennis Club Invitational Spring Lake, New Jersey; doubles (partner, Gardnar Mulloy)

Eastern Grass Court Championships Orange Lawn Tennis Club; South Orange, New Jersey; singles and doubles (partner, Gardnar Mulloy)

Newport Casino Lawn Tennis Club Invitational Newport, Rhode Island; doubles (partner, Gardnar Mulloy)

Pacific Southwest Championships Los Angeles Tennis Club; Los Angeles, California; doubles (partner, Pancho Segura)

Argentine Championships Buenos Aires Lawn Tennis Club; Buenos Aires, Argentina; singles and doubles (partner, Jaroslav Drobny)

1948   **River Oaks Country Club Invitational** Houston, Texas

Belgian Championships Royal Leopold Club; Brussels, Belgium; singles and doubles (partner, Budge Patty)

French Championships Stade Roland Garros Stadium; Paris, France

Eastern Clay Court Championships Jackson Heights Tennis Club; New York, New York

Seabright Tennis Club Invitational Seabright, New Jersey; doubles (partner, Bob Falkenburg)

Eastern Grass Court Championships Orange Lawn Tennis Club; South Orange, New Jersey

Newport Casino Lawn Tennis Club Invitational Newport, Rhode Island; doubles (partner, Ted Schroeder)

Pacific Southwest Championships Los Angeles Tennis Club; Los Angeles, California; doubles (partner, Ted Schroeder)

Pan-American Championships Centro Deportivo Chapultepec; Mexico City, Mexico; doubles (partner, Pancho Gonzales)

1949 **French Indoor Championships** Paris, France; singles and doubles (partner, Henri Cochet)

Egyptian Championships Gezira Sporting Club; Cairo, Egypt; singles and doubles (partner, Budge Patty)

Egyptian International Championships Alexandria Sporting Club; Alexandria, Egypt; singles and doubles (partner, Gottfried von Cramm)

Monte Carlo International Championships Monte Carlo Country Club; Monte Carlo, France

Paris Championships Stade Roland Garros Stadium; Paris, France

French Championships Stade Roland Garros Stadium; Paris, France; singles and doubles (partner, Pancho Gonzales)

Wimbledon All England Lawn Tennis & Croquet Club; Wimbledon, England; doubles (partner, Pancho Gonzales)

Spring Lake Bathing and Tennis Club Invitational Spring Lake, New Jersey

Pan-American Championships Centro Deportivo Chapultepec; Mexico City, Mexico

1937   **United States defeated Great Britain (4-1)** Wimbledon, England

Henry "Bunny" Austin (B) d. Frank Parker (US) (6-3, 6-2, 7-5)

Don Budge (US) d. Charlie Hare (B) (15-13, 6-1, 6-2)

Don Budge & Gene Mako (US) d. Charles Tuckey & Frank Wilde (B)
(6-3, 7-5, 7-9, 12-10)

Frank Parker *(US) d. Charlie Hare (B) (6-2, 6-4, 6-2)*

Don Budge (US) d. Henry "Bunny" Austin (B) (8-6, 3-6, 6-4, 6-3)

1938   **(Frank Parker did not play.)**

1939   **Australia defeated United States (3-2)** Haverford, Pennsylvania

Bobby Riggs (US) d. John Bromwich (A) (6-4, 6-0, 7-5)

Frank Parker *(US) d. Adrian Quist (A) (6-3, 2-6, 6-4, 1-6, 7-5)*

Adrian Quist & John Bromwich (A) d. Jack Kramer & Joe Hunt (US)
(5-7, 6-2, 7-5, 6-2)

Adrian Quist (A) d. Bobby Riggs (US) (6-1, 6-4, 3-6, 3-6, 6-4)

John Bromwich (A) d. **Frank Parker** *(US) (6-0, 6-3, 6-1)*

1940-45 **(not held)**

1946   **(Frank Parker played in the preliminary rounds only.)**

1947   **(Frank Parker did not play.)**

1948   **United States defeated Australia (5-0)** Forest Hills, New York

Frank Parker *(US) d. Bill Sidwell (A) (6-4, 6-4, 6-4)*

Ted Schroeder (US) d. Adrian Quist (A) (6-3, 4-6, 6-0, 6-0)

Bill Talbert & Gardnar Mulloy (US) d. Bill Sidwell & Colin Long (A)
(8-6, 9-7, 2-6, 7-5)

Ted Schroeder (US) d. Bill Sidwell (A) (6-2, 6-1, 6-1)

Frank Parker *(US) d. Adrian Quist (A) (6-2, 6-2, 6-3)*

U.S. Nationals★ (currently the U.S. Open) Scores for Frank Parker

1932   Defeated Sadakazu Onda in the 1st round (6-3, 7-5, 6-1)

Defeated Richard Murphy in the 2nd round (6-1, 6-2, 6-2)

Lost to George Lott in the 3rd round (6-4, 6-1, 4-6, 6-2)

1933   Defeated Giles Verstraten in the 1st round (6-3, 6-1, 6-2)

Defeated Frank Goeltz in the 2nd round (6-0, 6-2, 6-4)

Lost to Keith Gledhill in the 3rd round (4-6, 6-3, 11-9, 6-3)

1934   Bye in the 1st round

Defeated Edward Burns in the 2nd round by default

Defeated Robert Stanford in the 3rd round (6-2, 6-1, 6-2)

Defeated Roderich Menzel in the 4th round (8-6, 4-6, 3-6, 8-6, 6-3)

Lost to Sidney Wood in the quarterfinals (6-4, 6-4, 7-5)

1935   Bye in the 1st round

Defeated William Thompson in the 2nd round (6-0, 6-0, 4-6, 6-2)

Defeated Robert Bryan in the 3rd round (6-1, 6-1, 7-5)

Lost to Fred Perry in the 4th round (6-4, 6-2, 6-0)

1936   Bye in the 1st round

Defeated Manuel Alonso in the 2nd round (6-2, 6-2, 6-1)

Defeated Charles Harris in the 3rd round (6-4, 3-6, 6-1, 7-5)

Defeated Robert Harman in the 4th round (8-6, 6-2, 6-2)

Defeated Greg Mangin in the quarterfinals (10-12, 6-0, 4-6, 6-1, 6-3)

Lost to Don Budge in the semi-finals (6-4, 6-3, 6-3)

1937   Defeated William Gillespie in the 1st round (6-2, 6-1, 6-0)

Defeated Frank Bowden in the 2nd round (3-6, 6-2, 6-3, 6-1)

Defeated Gilbert Hunt in the 3rd round (6-1, 8-6, 6-1)

Defeated Sidney Wood in the 4th round (3-6, 4-6, 6-1, 6-3, 6-0)

Defeated Johnny Van Ryn in the quarterfinals (6-2, 12-10, 6-2)

Lost to Don Budge in the semi-finals (6-2, 6-1, 6-3)

★The U.S. Nationals was also called "The Nationals," "U.S. Championships," "National Championships," "U.S. Championship at Forest Hills," and "Forest Hills."

1938 Bye in the 1st round

Defeated William Lurie in the 2nd round (6-2, 6-1, 6-3)

Defeated Carlton Rood in the 3rd round (6-2, 6-4, 7-5)

Lost to John Bromwich in the 4th round (6-2, 6-3, 6-2)

1939 Defeated Amado Sanchez in the 1st round (6-0, 6-1, 6-1)

Defeated John Mahoney in the 2nd round (6-2, 6-4, 6-2)

Defeated Charles Hare in the 3rd round (6-4, 6-2, 3-6, 7-5)

Lost to Gilbert Hunt in the 4th round (6-1, 6-1, 6-1)

1940 Bye in the 1st round

Defeated P. Maguire in the 2nd round (6-3, 6-1, 7-5)

Defeated Thomas Kelly in the 3rd round (6-3, 6-1, 6-3)

Defeated William Gillespie in the 4th round (6-2, 6-3, 10-8)

Lost to Jack Kramer in the quarterfinals (1-6, 6-1, 3-6, 6-3, 6-1)

1941 Defeated Robert Kerdasha in the 1st round (6-1, 6-0, 6-3)

Defeated Edward Alloo in the 2nd round (6-2, 6-4, 6-1)

Defeated William Gillespie in the 3rd round (5-7, 6-1, 6-3, 7-5)

Lost to Bobby Riggs in the quarterfinals (6-4, 6-3, 4-6, 6-2)

1942 Defeated Jack Geller in the 1st round (6-0, 6-0, 6-0)

Defeated Richard Hart in the 2nd round (6-1, 6-3, 7-5)

Defeated William Vogt in the 3rd round (6-2, 6-0, 6-1)

Defeated Seymour Greenberg in the quarterfinals (6-0, 6-0, 6-4)

Defeated Pancho Segura in the semi-finals (6-1, 6-1, 2-6, 6-2)

Lost to Ted Schroeder in the finals (8-6, 7-5, 3-6, 4-6, 6-2)

1943 Defeated John Cushingham in the 1st round (6-2, 6-3)

Defeated David Freeman in the 2nd round (6-0, 6-4)

Lost to Joe Hunt in the quarterfinals (3-6, 6-2, 6-3)

1944 Defeated Bruce Thomas in the 1st round (6-0, 6-2)

Defeated Vic Seixas in the 2nd round (6-1, 6-4)

Defeated Charles Oliver in the quarterfinals (6-2, 6-4, 6-1)

Defeated Don McNeill in the semi-finals (6-4, 3-6, 6-2, 6-2)

Defeated Bill Talbert in the finals (6-4, 3-6, 6-3, 6-3)

1945   Bye in the 1st round

Defeated George Ball in the 2nd round (6-1, 6-2)

Defeated Rolor Ray in the 3rd round (6-1, 6-0)

Defeated Seymour Greenberg in the quarterfinals (6-2, 6-3, 6-2)

Defeated Elwood Cooke in the semi-finals (6-4, 8-6, 7-5)

Defeated Bill Talbert in the finals (14-12, 6-1, 6-2)

1946   Defeated Brendan Macken in the 1st round (6-1, 6-1, 6-3)

Defeated James Brink in the 2nd round (6-2, 6-1, 6-3)

Defeated Harry Likas in the 3rd round (6-0, 6-2, 6-3)

Defeated Seymour Greenberg in the 4th round (6-3, 6-3, 6-2)

Lost to Tom Brown in the quarterfinals (6-3, 6-4, 6-8, 3-6, 6-1)

1947   Defeated Clark Taylor in the 1st round (6-2, 6-1)

Defeated Ladislav Hecht in the 2nd round (6-2, 6-4, 6-4)

Defeated Bernard Destremau in the 3rd round (6-0, 6-2, 6-3)

Defeated Vic Seixas in the 4th round (6-1, 4-6, 6-3, 6-4)

Defeated Pancho Segura in the quarterfinals (6-3, 11-9, 6-4)

Defeated John Bromwich in the semi-finals (6-3, 4-6, 6-3, 6-8, 8-6)

Lost to Jack Kramer in the finals (4-6, 2-6, 6-1, 6-0, 6-3)

1948   Bye in the 1st round

Defeated Gilbert Bogley in the 2nd round (6-2, 6-1, 6-0)

Defeated John Lohstoeter in the 3rd round (6-0, 6-1, 6-0)

Defeated Frank Sedgman in the 4th round (6-4, 7-5, 6-3)

Lost to Pancho Gonzales in the quarterfinals (8-6, 2-6, 7-5, 6-3)

1949   Defeated Pierre Ganepele in the 1st round (6-2, 6-1, 6-1)

Defeated Charles Masterson in the 2nd round (6-2, 6-1, 6-1)

Defeated Eric Sturgess in the 3rd round (6-3, 6-8, 6-1, 6-4)

Defeated Gardnar Mulloy in the quarterfinals (6-4, 6-2, 6-4)

Lost to Pancho Gonzales in the semi-finals (3-6, 9-7, 6-3, 6-2)

1950-67 (Frank Parker did not play.)

1968   Bye in the 1st round

Lost to Arthur Ashe in the 2nd round (6-3, 6-2, 6-2)

1. Mercer Beasley, *How to Play Tennis: The Beasley System of Tennis Instruction* (New York: Garden City Publishing Company, Inc., 1933), 130.

2. George McGann, "Mercer Beasley," *The Fireside Book of Tennis*, edited by Allison Danzig and Peter Schwed (New York: Simon and Schuster, 1972), 273.

3. "Parker, as Unknown, Played Helen Wills," Unmarked clipping from Frank Parker's personal scrapbook.

4. *Jambalaya* (Tulane University Yearbook), 1934.

5. Bill Letwin, "Parker Won't Return to School; Tennis Claims All His Attention," *Milwaukee Journal*, 13 July 1937, sec. 2, p. 4.

6. *Olla Podrida* (Lawrenceville School Yearbook), 1934, 35, 36.

7. "Parker Weds Mrs. Beasley," *Milwaukee Journal*, 18 March 1938, sec. 2, p. 1.

8. Bill Letwin, "Frank's 'Babu,' Mother Listens to Radio With Prayers on Lips," *Milwaukee Journal*, 27 July 1937, sec. 2, p. 2.

9. Kenneth D. Fry, "Frank Parker is Junior Champion," *American Lawn Tennis*, 20 August 1932, 15–16.å

10. George M. Lott, Jr., "Parker is Canadian Champion," *American Lawn Tennis*, 20 August 1932, 20.

11. "Kentucky Title to Parker," *American Lawn Tennis*, 5 July 1933, 34.

12. Edward Hart, "Manufacturing a Tennis Champion," *Milwaukee Journal*, 13 August 1933, 7.

13. Stephen Wallis Merrihew, "The Editor's Talks with His Readers," *American Lawn Tennis*, 20 November 1935, 39.

14. Walter B. Schleiter, "Some Davis Cup Notes," *American Lawn Tennis*, 20 August 1937, 20.

15. Alice Marble, "Frank Parker Deserves a Break," *American Lawn Tennis*, 15 August 1947, 23.

16. R. G. Lynch, "Maybe I'm Wrong: The USLTA Must Do More Than Slap Wrists," *Milwaukee Journal*, 20 January 1942, sec. 2, p. 2.

17. Beasley, *How to Play Tennis: The Beasley System of Tennis Instruction*, 130, 125, 129, 2.

18. McGann, "Mercer Beasley," 273.

19. Will Grimsley, *Tennis: Its History, People and Events* (Englewood Cliffs: Prentice-Hall, 1971), 80.

20. Kevin Coyne, "The Frankie Parker Era," *Spring Lake Bath and Tennis Club 100-year Commemorative Book*, 1998, 14–15.

21. Jeane Hoffman, "Billy Talbert Continues Victory Sweep at Spring Lake," *American Lawn Tennis*, 1 September 1948, 10–11.

22. Coyne, "The Frankie Parker Era," 14.

23. U. P., "Joy to Parker, Beasley's Wish," *Milwaukee Journal*, 19 March 1938, sec. 1, p. 3.

24. Bill Letwin, "New Forehand, Confidence in His Own Ability, Spur Frank Parker in Tennis Comeback This Year," *Milwaukee Journal*, 25 June 1939, sec. 3, p. 3.

25. Jack Miller, "Parker Finally Wins Tri-State," *American Lawn Tennis*, 5 July 1941, 8.

26. "Eastern CCC at Jackson Heights," *American Lawn Tennis*, 20 July 1941, 4.

27. Edward C. Potter, Jr., "The Boy Made Good," *American Lawn Tennis*, October 1944, 36–37.

28. "Parker's Victory Returns Davis Cup to U.S. for First Time in 10 Years: Tennis Marvel of Milwaukee Defeats Briton," *Milwaukee Journal*, 27 July 1937, 1–2.

29. Walter B. Schleiter, "Some Davis Cup Notes," *American Lawn Tennis*, 20 August 1937, 20.

30. R. G. Lynch, "Maybe I'm Wrong: Parker Going to Coast to Get Ready for Riggs," *Milwaukee Journal*, 21 October 1937, sec.2, p. 8.

31. "Davis Cup Teamsters are Teetotal Benedicts," *New Zealand Free Lance*, 26 November 1946.

32. "Calls the Tune at Husband's Practice," Unmarked clipping from Frank Parker's personal scrapbook.

33. Gasper Octavio Almanza, "Parker and Segura—A Paragon," *American Lawn Tennis*, February 1946, 34.

34. "Parker Wins at Jackson Heights," *American Lawn Tennis*, 1 September 1946, 18.

35. Dick Squires, "Catching Up with…Frank Parker," *Tennis USTA: Supplement to Tennis Magazine*, August 1996, 4.

36. Alice Marble, "As I See It: Kramer, Gonzales & Co.," *American Lawn Tennis*, December, 1949, 26.

37. "The Half-Century In Tennis," *American Lawn Tennis*, February 1950, 15–16.

38. Photo caption, *American Lawn Tennis*, March 1951, 12.